HENRY COUNTY CEMETERIES [KENTUCKY]

Parts I, II, and III

by

Robert Foster Johnson

and

Willada Rickman Dent

(Mrs. Paul L. Dent)

CLEARFIELD

Originally published in
The Filson Club History Quarterly
Louisville, Kentucky

Henry County Cemeteries: Part I
Volume 52, No. 3, July 1978, pp. 280–303

Henry County Cemeteries: Part II
Volume 52, No. 4, October 1978, pp. 340–362

Henry County Cemeteries: Part III
Volume 53, No. 3, July 1979, pp. 250–297

Reprinted with the permission of
The Filson Club

Reprinted in one volume for
Clearfield Company, Inc., by
Genealogical Publishing Co., Inc.
Baltimore, Maryland
2006

International Standard Book Number: 0-8063-5315-5

Made in the United States of America

HENRY COUNTY CEMETERIES [KENTUCKY]

Part I

by
Robert Foster Johnson

HENRY COUNTY CEMETERIES: PART I

By Robert Foster Johnson*

1. Kerlin Graveyard, John Acree, owner.
Jericho Road, 2½ m. E of LaGrange.

KERLIN, Mattie	d. of S. & M. Kerlin	6-20-1860	10- 1-1862
, Lucinda		5- 7-1836	9-18-1879

2. Kelso Graveyard, Don Lutz, owner.
Jericho Road, 2½ m. E of LaGrange.

KELSO, W. T.		2-17-1840	3-29-1884
, Tommie		5-13-1881	9-14-1884

3. Smith Cemetery, Bradley, owner.
Between Hwy. 146, LaGrange, and Jericho roads.

BAXTER, G. D.		1884	1925
, Isabella P.	w. of G. D. a. 38 y.		4-13-1886
SMITH, I. M.	husband	1836	1902
, E. M.	wife	1839	1903
, Ballard S.		8-26-1813	7- 7-1883
, Julia	w. of Ballard	9-19-1816	10-13-1851
, Eliza J.		1- 2-1833	8-24-1856
, Eliza	w. of Russell M. a. 45 y., 5 m., 20 d.		2- 9-1850
, Russel	s. of John & Mary S.	5- 1-1801	8-25-1851
B. A. S.			
SMITH, James B.	b. Henry Co., Ky.	11-20-1807	8-25-1851
, Mary S.	w. of John a. 63 y.		3- 9-1847
, John	s. of Park Smith of Va.		
, John B.	s. of John B. & Susan E. a. 16 y., 5 m., 21 d.		5-17-1841
, William Adams		5-28-1829	4-23-1911
, Emily	w. of W. A.	2-14-1837	7- 9-1875
, Louisa E.	w. of Isaac W.	6-21-1839	3-27-1879
, John Park		6-10-1803	5-25-1883
, Susannah E.	w. of John Park married 2-5-1824	10-21-1802	10-23-1870
, Isaac W., Jr.	a. 27 y. killed on L. S. Railroad		11- 8-1893
, Frank		1868	1894
, Alice H.	d. of Isaac M. & Eliza M.	12-25-1864	5-13-1873

4. Mt. Olivet Baptist Church Cemetery.
Lane, N. LaGrange, Jericho Road.

BARRICKMAN, Gina Rin	d. of L. & C. B.	3-10-1861	7- 7-1864

---

*Robert Foster Johnson, M.A., is a native of Casey County and taught history for many years at Shawnee High School in Louisville. He is one of the founders of the Oldham County Historical Society.

Abbreviations: a., age; b., born; c., child; d., daughter, days; h., husband; m., married, miles, months; s., son; w., wife; y., years. The second part of this article will be published in a future issue. This is not an exhaustive list of all Henry County cemeteries. A space where a date should be indicates that the information is not on the tombstone.

HOLMES, Sarah Stark	d. of S. & S. T.	7-11-1861	7-20-1861
, Stark		8-23-1820	7- 5-1890
, Sarah Theresa	w. of Stark	2-21-1819	
PENDLETON, Isaac T.		2-22-1811	1- 3-1865
ROBBINS, Abel		12-27-1779	5-18-1866
, Mary D.	w. of Abel	4-23-1782	8-17-1866
, Charity	d. of Abel & Mary D.	3- 4-1811	8- 4-1853
ROBINS, Margaret A.	consort of Geo. H.	8-28-1823	1-12-1851
WATKINS, Stephen	in 78th y.		2-23-1863
, David		2-19-1777	3-20-1864
, Prudence	a. 84 y., 11 m.		3-23-1866

5. Smith, Sibley, Bibb Cemetery, Mr. Case, owner.
250 yds. N of Mt. Olivet Baptist Church Cemetery, #4.

ALLEN, Nora Bain	d. of B. H. & M. E. a. 7 m., 15 d.		3-15-1871
SIBLEY, Catherine Bibb	w. of John	3-31-1803	3- 7-1872
, John	b. Prince Edward Co., Va. d. Trimble Co., Ky.	12- 7-1797	8-14-1877
SMITH, F. A.		11- 5-1809	9- 4-1866
, Elizabeth M.	w. of F. A.	2-21-1819	5-29-1852
, John Russell		3-16-1824	2-13-1862
, Esther Eliz.	d. of G. R. & E. N.	3-10-1856	3- 5-1859
, Thomas		5-10-1778	1-23-1846
, Thomas Sr.	b. Louisa Co., Va.	5-11-1778	-23-1816
, Marcellus		10-21-1819	2-13-1840
WADE, Eliz. Quarles	w. of E. F.		12-13-1861
, Neville	s. of E. F. & E. Q.	7-31-1849	7-31-1849

6. Houseworth Graveyard, Forest Bramblett, owner.
Same Lane as #4 & #5, 400 yds. E Hwy. 146.

BICKNELL, Wm. W.	s. of S. H. & N. S.	3-22-1862	1-18-1874
, Robt. L.	s. of S. H. & N. S.	11- 8-1864	2- 8-1868
HOUSEWORTH, Eliz. P.	w of Elisha	4-23-1800	12-28-1874
, Elisha		11- 3-1803	
, Mary E.	d. of E. & E. P.	12- 3-1835	8-20-1887
, Mary	w. of Henry		12-30-1833

7. Vance Graveyard, D. C. Ward, owner,
3 m. E of LaGrange on Hwy. 146.

VANCE, Robert	s. of R. W. & Virginia R.	8-15-1849	3-25-1896
, Thomas S.	s. of R. W. & Sue	4-23-1876	11- 8-1892
, Thomas S.	shot at LaGrange 7-27-1876 a. 22 y., 11 m., 7 d	8-22-1853	7-29-1876
, Ferdinand C.	s. of R. W. & Virginia R.	11-14-1867	9-17-1880
, Virginia R.	w. of R. W., Sr.	4-30-1827	2-22-1887
, R. W., Sr.		10-27-1817	1-29-1890
, Chas. M.		8- 3-1851	4-20-1914
, Albert B.	s. of R. W. & Virginia	10-23-1857	4-27-1886

8. Hendronville Graveyard.
Pendleton-Jericho Road, 1 m. N of Jericho

BROWNING, Octavia	w. of John	12- 7-1812	10-21-1880
DODD, Geo. H.		9-13-1817	7-18-1864
, Nancy	d. of Geo. H. & Lorinda A.	12- 5-1848	10-18-1859
EDDY, Alex.		2-20-1800	7-21-1846
HENSON, Nancy	w. of James	2-23-1802	1-29-1881
, James		10-29-1801	3-11-1887
HENTON, Hannah	w. of Casper a. 54 y., 6 m., 17 d.		10-17-1847
JOHNSON, Jessee		2- 9-1836	2- 9-1866

LEMASTER, Polly		4-17-1802	3-12-1879
, Wesley		5-10-1792	3-17-1858
LANE, Joseph C.		1-30-1827	9-24-1860
REED, Johnnie	Ky. Cpl. — 814 Pioneer Inf.	4- 1-1894	1- 4-1945
THOMPSON, John W.	s. of J. C. & B.	9-15-1825	8-24-1853
, James		12-15-1785	12-20-1847
, Amasa		1-21-1802	4- 5-1879
WALROND, Mary B.	w. of H. C. a. 30 y		12-10-1848
WILLETT, Nancy D.	w. of Dr. G. F.	4- 7-1828	8-31-1860
WINBURN, A. J.	s. of Lemuel & Lucy a. 64 y.		2-11-1892

9. Jenkins - Adcock Cemetery.
4 m. N of Campbellsburg, jct. U.S. Hwy. 55 & 316.

ADCOCK,	infant s. of E. A. & Spillbury	5- 3-1876	6- 3-1876
, Emily Alice	w. of Spillbury	3- 2-1855	12- 4-1879
JENKINS, Emily M.	w. of W. H.	10-22-1825	2- 7-1857
, James R.		9-26-1846	4-17-1869
, Elizabeth	w. of J. S. a. 102 y., 8 m.		5-15-1892
, Emily M.	w. of W. H.	10-22-1825	2- 7-1857
, J. S.		11-26-1795	8-17-1884
, Wm. H.		9-26-1823	2-16-1898
McDOWELL, Sarah E.		1-15-1808	4-10-1882

10. Pryor Graveyard, owner, Phillip Powell.
1 m. SW of New Castle, 1 m. S of Hwy. 146.

Capt. Jack Pryor

11. Browning - Land Cemetery
Jct. Hwy. 1606 & 146.

BROWNING, Rachel May	1889	1963
, Evan H.	1892	1960
, Hazel Tiller	1897	19--
, Cabel B.	1866	1951
, Susan M.	1871	1955
LAND, Evan	1839	1920
, Rachael	1843	1922
, J. R.	1874	1900

12. Moore Graveyard.
2 m. W of #11 on Hwy. 146.

MOORE, Margaret	w. of T. J.	3-15-1807	10-19-1853
, P. C.		8-15-1896	7- 4-1898
, Clarence C.		6-14-1892	9-30-1892
, J. H.		1849	1897

13. Smithfield Public Cemetery.
By Smithfield Baptist Church.

ABRAHAM, J. Newton		9-18-1857	5- 1-1940
, Dixie V.	w. of J. N.	7-22-1858	9-30-1916
ADAMS, A. J.		1844	1911
, M. J.	w. of A. J.	1850	1931
ALLEN, Ben T.		1867	1946
, Fred		3- 2-1868	5-29-1903
, Benjamin H. D.		8- 8-1824	11- 2-1903

Name	Note	Born	Died
ATCHISON, William	husband	1838	1920
, Fannie W.	wife	1842	1929
, Harriet		12-20-1810	1-31-1896
, Hugh		3-15-1811	5-27-1875
BARBOUR, William E.		6-25-1819	10-10-1902
, Harriett R.	w. of Wm. E.	7- 4-1824	6-22-1896
BARRACKMAN, Isaac	husband	10-11-1823	4- 1-1885
Catherine A.	wife	4-21-1839	1-22-1872
BATE, James Smalley		1863	1939
, Nell Moss	w. of J. S.	1874	1935
BERRY, Henry D.	s. of E. T.	1867	1924
, Joel H.		5-24-1835	1-13-1900
BLAKEMORE, Joseph Wm.	husband	3- 7-1840	12-28-1905
, Araminta Owen	wife	12-29-1844	7-11-1915
, J. Neville	a. 58 y.		1-30-1863
, Mary Moxley	w. of J. N. a. 78 y.		3-19-1899
BOHANNON, W. A.		11-17-1833	11- 9-1903
, Mary E.	w. of W. A.	1- 1-1835	8-12-1912
BOYER, Sallie C.		5-29-1834	12-28-1907
BRIGHT, J. D.		1850	1930
, Hallie S.		1853	1940
BRYANT, R. D.		1836	1926
, Sarah E.	w. of R. D.	1840	1878
BURCH, Daniel	a. 73 y.		5-19-1883
, Mahala	w. of Daniel	1808	8-29-1879
CALLAWAY, William Edwin	father	1836	1868
, Martha O.	mother	1840	1922
, Elizabeth	w. of William	5-16-1813	4-21-1882
, Orville		1850	1908
, Jennie		1855	1936
CALLIS, Cerelda B.		8-25-1843	5-28-1917
, Samuel G.		1864	1940
CHOATE, George W.		6-12-1842	2-15-1902
, Mittie Mitchell		12-25-1842	12-31-1908
CLAXON, James R.		1850	1926
CLIFFORD, Sallie M. Woods	w. of B. F. a. 24 y., 5 m., 12 d.		8-30-1872
CLORE, James W.		1841	1913
CONSTANTINE, James		1-15-1810	7-13-1888
, Casander F. Moore	w. of James	3- 1-1826	7- 4-1898
CORBIN, Belle		1849	1922
CRABB, Mildred A.	w. of J. P.	3-10-1833	9- 6-1880
, J. P.		1- 1-1825	1- 5-1896
DAVIS, Joseph Barnhill		1853	1936
, Warren	husband a. 98 y.		11-15-1875
, Jane	wife a. about 82 y		7-11-1864
DeJARNETTE, Hannah Tribble		1819	1905
DOYLE, Nelson C.		1842	1925
, Annie M.	w. of N. C.	1839	1928
, George		2-28-1798	2-20-1861
, Elizabeth	w. of George	9-14-1805	12-12-1878
, Alice Vories		1844	1878
, George W.		1840	1907
, Pauline		1850	1930
DRANE, G. F.		1864	1902
, Richard Bate		6-14-1897	12- 9-1898
, Eady	w. of T. S.	4-11-1799	4-25-1877
, Theodore S.		10-27-1796	2- 7-1869
, B. F.		1822	1902
, Mary E.	w. of B. F.	1833	1913
, Ona Moore	w. of T. S. a. 24 y., 3 m., 10 d.		5-26-1865
, Ida K.	wife	1860	1950
, James N.	husband	1858	1933
, Charles E.		1866	1929
, S. T., Jr.		6- 6-1820	11- 1-1894
, Ruth Ellen	w. of S. T.	3- 3-1830	6- 6-1906

EATON, James Mason		7-30-1833	7-23-1912
ENGEL, Maymie Allan		1872	1923
FAWKES, George W.	husband	1852	1934
, Mary W.	wife	1854	1935
, George W.		5- 7-1880	9-25-1940
FIELD, Wm. Walker	husband		
, Susan Gilbert	w. of W. W.		
GATES, Fannie Blakemore	w. of Sidney J.	1857	1904
GIVIDEN, John		11-29-1825	3-25-1873
, Matilda J.	w. of John	5-17-1826	1-21-1903
, F. P.		1852	1914
, Bela Willett		3-19-1854	5- 5-1890
GLASCOCK, Dr. Harvey W.		1857	1941
, Della M.	w. of Dr. H. W.	1877	1938
GOODRIDGE, Elizabeth	w. of F. H.	11- 2-1809	8- 8-1864
, F. H.		3-21-1804	6-14-1869
, F. H., Jr.		6- 7-1843	12- 2-1862
, John C.		2-17-1827	9-20-1856
HAGGARD, Mary Sanford		1843	1913
, David D.		7-28-1812	12-14-1880
, Temperance	w. of D. D.	12-28-1811	4-28-1883
HARRIS, Margaret		11-12-1838	1-10-1911
HAYS, William S.		6-27-1868	7-24-1946
, Minnie Field		4- 1-1870	2-10-1956
, William G.		5- 4-1837	3- 4-1920
, Mildred E.	w. of W. G.	5-30-1840	4-28-1905
, Arthur Y.		1880	1942
HEAD, Stella Tandy		12-12-1887	1-28-1969
, Charles E.		2-11-1874	3-10-1938
, Gellie Y.		10-11-1888	2-24-1961
HENSLEY, Willie Francis	w. of Thos. P.	8-27-1869	3-22-1918
HIEATT, Martha Tribble	w. of Wm.	1820	1901
HILL, William L.		5- 1-1808	2-10-1864
, Amanda S.		4- 9-1816	1-19-1891
HINKLE, William		1805	1859
, Sallie	w. of Wm.		1893
HOUSEWORTH, Florence E.		1876	1919
, Elizabeth M.		1839	1921
, Spotwood H.		1833	1915
, E. P.	husband	1843	1932
, E. A.		1847	1921
HURLEY, Thomas J.		11-23-1837	8- 7-1895
JACKSON, James		1793	1870
, Emily T.		1812	1890
, Jesse M.		11- 4-1849	10-13-1886
, James A.		10-24-1842	10-30-1878
, Eliza B.		1842	1929
, Sallie V.		1860	1921
, Benjamin F.		1847	1921
JOHANTGEN, John Frank		1857	1944
, Leni Lamaster		1861	1941
KEPHART, Anna S.		1855	1937
LaMASTER, Willie Hugh		1863	1868
LEWIS, F. E.		1839	7-12-1919
, Martha M.	w. of F. E.	2-18-1843	4-13-1913
, Amanda	a. 50 y.		9-15-1881
MADDOX, Jane		12-11-1797	12-30-1870
MEADE, Iverson G.		1852	1944
, Kate DeJarnette	w. of I. G.	1858	1947
, DeJarnette		1889	1915
MITCHELL, B. S.		7-16-1810	11-14-1874
, Mary D.		11- 6-1817	1- 3-1892
MONTAGUE, Mollie J.	w. of B.	1872	1917
, Byron		1865	1941
MOODY, Rumenah B.		8-15-1817	9- 5-1871
MOORE, M. George	husband	1861	1929
, Eddie G.	wife	1864	1961
, Mariam R.	w. of Maples B.	1- 7-1797	4- 8-1869
, Maples		11-22-1798	7-19-1859
MORRIS, James C.		1843	1920

, Mary E.	w. of James C.	1848	1923
MOXLEY, William B.		1-25-1794	1-27-1872
McALLISTER, Daniel A.		1832	1917
, Sarah E.	w. of D. A.	1836	1899
, R. A.		2-10-1872	2-10-1935
, Dixie		1865	1948
, J. S.		1833	1923
, Sallie	w. of J. S.	1848	1927
, Lillie		1875	1953
McBURNEY, Fannie L.	w. of W. O.		
McCANN, James		4- 6-1811	2-17-1875
, Sarah Gott		1831	1865
NEAL, Rebecca J.		1-12-1852	9-18-1915
, George M.		1858	1948
NEBLETT, Annie T.	w. of Thos. E.	1866	1958
, Thomas E.		1865	1941
NETHERTON, James P.		1852	1933
, Sallie	w. of J. P.	1862	1960
NOE, Elam P.		4-23-1858	3- 4-1934
, Fannie	w. of E. P.	7-17-1858	4- 5-1935
OLDHAM, George D.		2-14-1846	2-14-1922
OWEN, John	a. 64 y., 8 m., 13 d.		1-30-1871
PARKHURST, G. A.	husband	1856	1928
A. B. Vance	w. of G. A.	1862	1940
PATTERSON, Anna Mae Meade		1881	1917
PERRY, John S.	husband	11-18-1820	10-28-1898
, Elizabeth	w. of J. S.	10-12-1831	2-16-1916
PREWITT, Marion A.	w. of R. C.	4-14-1845	10-18-1870
, Horace B.		6-14-1845	10- 5-1885
RADFORD, Henry D.	s. of John & Louisa	12-12-1847	1-18-1871
, John		1-28-1812	5-16-1901
, Louisa		1-28-1823	1-21-1910
RIDGEWAY, G. D.		2-13-1845	12-27-1943
ROCKWELL, Florence, M.		3- 7-1861	11- 4-1910
, Oker G.		1892	1966
, James I.		1888	1925
SANFORD, Milly	w. of Henry	1-29-1815	11- 1-1847
, James T.		1- 4-1846	8-10-1875
, Sarah E.	w. of H. M.	2-19-1834	3- 7-1907
, Henry M.		8-15-1807	11-13-1867
SIBLEY, James B.		1847	1924
, Nora J.		1873	1950
, Nora		4- 2-1839	2-17-1902
SMITH, Zhale		3-30-1874	8- 6-1957
, Wm. N.		2-20-1822	10-19-1866
, E. J.	w. of W. N.	11-21-1831	12-17-1881
, Elizabeth		8-27-1812	2-10-1872
, William V		7- 3-1863	4- 5-1932
, Nettie	w. of W. V.	12-14-1863	10-15-1922
SPURGEON, Benjamin F.	in 63rd y.		3- 8-1864
, Louisa	w. of B. F.	4- 9-1807	2- 9-1880
, Mattie DeJarnett		1848	1927
SWAIN, Dr. John		3- 4-1808	10-15-1900
, Mary E.	w. of Dr. J. B.	5-31-1814	5-27-1882
TANDY, Oscar M.		1868	1923
, Sallie W.	w. of O. M.	1871	1935
TEMME, August		2-18-1853	12-29-1901
, Frederick A.		1827	1895
Christiana		1822	1894
THOMPSON, Lemuel		5- 2-1795	2-21-1865
TIDRICK, R. L.		7-17-1837	4-11-1906
, Minta Hill	w. of R. L.		
TINSLEY, James		6-15-1821	12-23-1862
, Evilie	w. of James	12- 1-1823	1-10-1878
, John	a. 94 y.		3- 4-1871
, Lucy G.	w. of John	2- 2-1783	1-12-1863
, Dr. J. J.	a. 56 y.		1- 6-1875
, Cora B.		1863	1931
, Granville		1819	1858
, Deliah	w. of Granville	1823	1892

WATKINS, Squire		5- 5-1809	11-19-1872
, Huldah	w. of Squire	5-11-1816	7-23-1892
, John Evan	husband	1837	1926
, Rachel		1839	1890
, John H.		3-20-1861	6-27-1905
, Sallie Bet		1860	1924
, George Thomas		1854	1924
WILDER, Joe	husband	1908	1966
, Anna Martha	w. of Joe	1912	1967
WINGFIELD, Lovick Marvin		8-20-1883	1-20-1908
, Susanna Ellis		12-19-1846	11-27-1910
WOODS, Virginia	w. of I. M.	12-11-1838	1-29-1889
, I. M.		1821	1901
WOOLFOLK, John Franklin		1848	1928
, Mary E.		1879	
VORIES, William L.		10-29-1817	6- 6-1910
, Sarah Scott	w. of William L.	6-14-1821	5-23-1900

14. Sulphur Public Cemetery.
2 m. SE of Sulphur on Hwy. 1606.

ADAMS, John T.		1849	1938
, Lena R.		11- 6-1862	3- 4-1908
BROYLES, John W.	husband	1862	1937
, Susie B.	wife	1870	1948
BURTON, William		1862	1943
, Jefferson Davis		4- 6-1817	11-13-1890
CAMPBELL, Cordie M.	w. of J. W.	9- 8-1876	11-16-1905
CAPLINGER, S. D.		2-13-1830	1- 9-1913
, Sue J.	w. of S. D.	7- 1-1845	6- 9-1902
CLARK, James W.	husband	10- 5-1850	8-22-1910
, Martha J.		4- 3-1850	4-30-1924
COLEMAN, J. J.	husband	1869	1942
, Nora L. Morris	w. of J. J.	1868	1935
DEAN, Annie Burton		1859	1945
, Pryor H.	husband	1872	1943
, Alice C.	wife	1870	1931
FORD, Julia Penn		1882	19--
, Stanton		1878	1962
FOREE, Francis Marion	husband	1843	1930
, Harriett Foote	wife	1845	1920
GARNETT, A. C.		1847	1915
, Kate W.	w. of A. C.	1859	1925
GIVIDEN, Benj. F.		1849	1895
, Andrew J.	husband	12-11-1854	3-23-1936
, Georgia A.	w. of A. J.	5- 8-1860	5- 8-1930
GREENWOOD, John D.		1845	1925
, Dorcas M.	w. of J. D.	1858	1930
HANCOCK, Dr. F. D.		1874	1957
, Ethyl F.		1879	1927
KIDWELL, George M.		1865	1936
, Melissa		1870	1939
LOGAN, Mattie		1881	1947
McILVAINE, Sue Elliott		1897	1968
MARTIN, Dr. Charles Robert		1842	1915
, Minnie R.	w. of Dr. C. R		
MERCHANT, William P., Jr		1888	1960
, Lucy Y.	w. of W. P.	1890	
MOODY, James L.	husband	1853	1928
, Minnie E.	wife	1865	1906
MORRIS, W. B.		1823	1900
, Bettie	w. of W. B.	1832	1900
, Dr. Wm. Joseph	husband	1844	1922
, Mildred Haggard	w. of Dr. W. J.	1850	1921
PENN, Henry		1842	1919
PEYTON, Wm. Thomas	husband	1870	1926
, Polly Ann	wife	1871	1943
RALSTON, Minnie C.		1885	1960

ROCKWELL, W. Felix		1835	1912
, Mervin W.		1865	1927
SHOUSE, W. T.		1848	1937
, Nannie F		1868	1912
SHRADER, J. Albert		11- 2-1830	9-25-1903
, Malvina G.	w. of J. A.	4-17-1848	9- 8-1931
, J. W.		12-14-1849	3- 4-1887
SMITH, J. J.	husband	2-20-1839	11- 5-1901
, Kate	w. of J. J.	10- 8-1841	12-29-1925
SPILLMAN, Frank		1848	1922
, Arminda	w. of F.	1856	1910
STIVERS, Lewis C.		1857	1942
, Joanna Booth	wife of L. C.	1859	1927
THOMPSON, A. J.		10-23-1803	7-21-1875
WALKER, L. D.		1860	1901
, Wm. H.		1819	1893
, Sarah		1825	1909
WINBURN, William		1862	1931
, Virginia	w. of Wm.	1862	1932
WORK, Lionel		1894	

15. Old Kalfus Graveyard, Chester Adams. owner
400 yds. S of Bates Rd., 2 m. E of Pendleton.

ARNOLD, James T.	a. 50 y		
BLACK, Sallie	w. of John S.	7- 2-1836	3-22-1866
, James		3- 6-1799	8-11-1858
, Mary G.		2-14-1801	8- 1-1858
, James W.		12-23-1835	3-26-1864
HULETT, Milton	49th y.		8-13-1877
, Lucinda F.	w. of Milton	9- 4-1825	1-22-1879

16. 1 m. N of Hwy. 146 and branch of Little Ky. River. On ridge 4-5 m. SE of Pendleton.

MORRIS, Samuel T.			1874
, William J.	s. of S. T. & J.	1851	1861
, Thornton		2-15-1828	
, Mary V.	w. of W. B.	1-24-1827	9- 8-1874
STRAUGHAN, William J. N.			9-20-1854

(Also several small markers.)

17. Morris Graveyard.
N of Hwy. 157 between New Castle and Sulphur, 150 yds. E of Sulphur Public Cemetery

MORRIS, Lena R.		5- 9-1870	9- 9-1946
, David		6- 2-1819	10-30-1895
, Amanda M.	w. of David	3-14-1827	4-13-1910
, J. A.		1-30-1849	6-27-1912
, Nannie B.	w. of J. A.	3-26-1856	1-14-1902
, Sallie A.	w. of H. H.	4-30-1856	3-26-1893

18. Bates Road, 1½ m. N of Jericho, near Little Ky. River bank.

WHITELEY, Jennie	w. of A.	6-12-1794	3-23-1832

(Stone in pieces — may belong to another grave.)

19. Watkins Graveyard, J. H. Whaley, owner
On Giltner Lane, 2 m. SE of Smithfield.

WATKINS, Evan	b. Jan (April?) 18		1- 7-1831

Bronze Rev. War marker placed by Bland Ballard Chapter, D. A. R

20. 1 m. S of Smithfield on Hwy. 322.

Name	Note	Born	Died
BATES, Elizabeth	a. 40 y.		3-19-1812
DEAN, Louisa	w. of Jonathon	1807	1856
DURRETT, William L.		12-30-1821	11- 3-1888
MITCHELL, Elizabeth	w. of J. G.	10-30-1813	5- 1-1907
, J. G.		12-10-1802	7- 5-1885
, Charles		2- 3-1832	8-10-1853
, Martha		10-27-1837	8- 3-1853
, Robert D.		4- 3-1853	7- 9-1853
, Mary		11-18-1835	7- 7-1853
, Henry G.		3-22-1846	7-11-1853
, Mrs. Mary		1- 1-1779	9- 4-1843

21. Old Tanner Graveyard, C. M. Browning, owner.
1½ m. W of Jericho, 300 yds. E of State Road.

Name	Note	Born	Died
TANNER, Ellen		2-11-1817	12- 3-1892
, Wesley	s. of B. F. & E.	4- 9-1846	4- 8-1877
, Alice	d. of B. F. & E.	11-29-1858	4-29-1860
, Mary Ellen	d. of B. F. & E.		10-18-1859
, John H.	s. of B. F. & E.	10-26-1856	10-18-1859

22. Old Ladd Farm.
Near Oldham-Henry County line.

Name	Note	Born	Died
MILTON, Mary F.	d. of R. J. & E. A.	4- 3-1853	7- 8-1853

23. New Castle Public Cemetery.
1½ m. N of New Castle.

Name	Note	Born	Died
ALLNUTT, Rebecca F. Johnson		1862	1931
BATTS, Jessie	husband	10-14-1866	7-25-1900
, Ella	wife	1-27-1868	8- 5-1929
BOONE, Ann S. Bryan Perry		8- 7-1789	1-23-1887
	m. E. R. Perry 3-4-1816		
	2nd m. Wm. S. Boone		
BOURNE, Anne Shanks	w. of H. K.		1958
, Henry Kirby	s. of Thos. J. & Sarah	1862	1935
BOYER, Sanford Marion	husband	1868	1933
, Cynthia Evans	wife	1872	1957
BRENT, Dr. Sanford		7- 5-1800	4-21-1892
, Nancy	w. of Dr. S.	8-23-1807	7-12-1889
BRUCE, John		1834	1909
, Anna		1849	1917
, John D.	Ky. Pvt., Army, WW I	7-27-1893	12-26-1967
, Mary Roberts		10- -1844	5- -1881
CAPLINGER, William Allen		1859	1897
, James Nelson		1828	1896
, Amanthis		1835	1906
, Ann		1861	1945
, Emma Nelson		1867	1885
CARR, Lindsay		11-28-1877	4-24-1898
, Melissa		6-12-1847	3-11-1924
CARROLL, John D.		1854	1927
, John S.		1900	1932
, Lewis Charles		1905	1946
, Hallie Sanford	w. of J. D.	1876	1936
, William		11- 9-1836	3- 2-1909
, Mary J.		9-21-1842	1- 3-1922
, Dr. Owen	husband	1871	1947
, Francis P.	w. of Dr. O.	1872	1938
CHRISTIAN, Marion	husband	1890	1962
, Agnes	wife	1889	1967
, William L.		1859	1937
, Loulie E.		1866	1938

, Marion W.	husband	5-15-1827	2-20-1898
, Amanda D.	wife	8-19-1835	1-18-1914
COLLINS, Mary C.		1854	1929
, Ellen		1862	1941
John D.		1828	1908
DEAN, Ehrman E.	husband	1873	1959
, Sophia B.	wife	1874	1958
DIXON, Mollie M.		1855	1917
, John W.		1856	1926
DOUGLAS, John		1849	1927
DOUGLASS, Hallie B.		1862	1949
DOUTHITT, Stonewall Jackson	husband	1861	1951
, Nannie Samuel		1865	1939
ELLIS, Eliza B.		1813	1896
, James P.		1801	1893
, Jane B.		1806	1888
, Anna P.		1844	1926
, Berry		4-19-1804	11- 6-1878
, Thos. H.		1-18-1842	11- 6-1861
FEARS, Jesse	husband	1833	1883
, Elizabeth	wife	1834	1923
FOREE, Peter G.		4- 6-1851	1-21-1884
, Susan Roberts	w. of Thos. P.	7-13-1832	1-23-1879
, Peter	husband	6- 4-1783	10- 2-1881
, Nancy		2- 9-1784	8-17-1879
GIST, William L.	husband	5-29-1829	11-23-1895
, Bettie H.	wife	1- 1-1836	12-26-1909
GIVIDEN, William Thos.	husband	1867	1951
, Eva McMannis	w. of W. T.	1872	1922
GUTHRIE, Robert S.	husband	1840	1916
, Bettie Corbin		1840	1911
HARROD, Caroline	a. 77 y.		7-19-1895
HERNDON, Mary	w. of Henry	6-24-1818	8- 3-1864
HICKS, John	husband	1854	1914
, Mary E.		1855	1933
JACKSON, William O.		1864	1933
JAMES, Donald C.		1926	
KEPHART, Isaac Stuart		1887	1917
LaMASTER, Z. H.	husband	10-12-1860	6- 8-1938
, Minerva C.	w. of Z. H.	10-29-1867	3-30-1951
LANDERS, Mildred M.		1904	1950
, Lt. Col. Erle H.		1903	1951
LONG, John W.	husband	1864	1934
, Sarah B.	wife	1876	1934
McLEOD, Rev. L. T.	"Our Pastor"	4-10-1850	2- 4-1882
MARTINIE, Ella B.		1876	1938
MATHEWS, John W.		1843	1896
, Geo. B.		1876	1898
MORGAN, Susan E.		1868	1952
, A. Sid		1867	1950
MORRIS, H. H.		1846	1918
, Anne Y.		1850	1914
NUTTALL, Dr. W. L.	a. 76 y.		6-28-1920
, Alice C.	a. 82 y.		8-20-1933
OLDHAM, Robert Pryor		1885	1885
, Nannie Pryor		1861	1889
, Dr. Wm. B		10 -7-1832	8-18-1877
, Laura A.		1841	1896
, Dr. Geo. P.		1858	1933
PATTON, John Harrison		1917	1933
PERRY, M. B.	husband	1818	1896
, Narcissa	wife	1828	1905
PRYOR, Samuel Morton		1853	1953
, Mary Brinker		1824	1854
, Wm. Samuel		1825	1914
, Apphia, Beasley		1835	1895
, Joseph		1868	1911
, Mary Marshall	w. of Jos.	1877	1951
, Apphia Phelps		1-16-1903	7-28-1967
ROBERTS, Geo. W.	husband	1877	1943

Name	Note	Born	Died
, Scottie R.	wife	1882	
, Moten B.		7-19-1851	3-13-1876
, Laura		3-11-1853	3-13-1865
, Amanda	wife	10- 8-1816	7-18-1901
, John T.		10-16-1814	1- 1-1864
SANFORD, L. Major	husband	1824	1901
, Fannie	wife	1846	1892
SCEARCE, Ruhamah E.		1837	1923
SCOBEE, James C.		5-14-1840	5- 9-1911
SCOTT, Owen C.		1891	1940
, Lev. Thompson	husband	1864	1923
, Anna Belle	wife	1894	1911
SHANNON, O. C.		2-20-1886	
SMITH, Thomas		11-22-1790	8- 7-1850
, John Shrader		1886	1960
, Lucy L.		1891	1968
, Park		1858	1920
, Mary E.		1865	1928
, Leslie K.		10-30-1855	3-20-1916
, Virginia A.		1856	1925
, C. A., Sr.		1849	1926
STIVERS, Virginia Scott		1897	1968
, Oscar W.	husband	1873	1930
, Lou	wife	1877	1966
TURNER, Wm. Wirt		1844	1932

24. Center Street Cemetery.
Center Street, New Castle.

Name	Note	Born	Died
BROWN, Nannie W.		11-11-1834	1- 1-1864
, Elizabeth		8-14-1822	3-12-1867
, Anderson		7-24-1832	9- 6-1863
, Thomas		7-24-1790	3-25-1865
, Nancy	consort of Thos. in 61st y.		6-26-1854
BUCKLEY, Martha	w. of H. M. d. of Joseph M. & Martha Thomasson	2-19-1825	
GRAY, Julia S.	d. of R. B. & Elizabeth	12-20-1835	1-11-1860
HERNDON, John G.	b. Scott Co., Ky.	7-16-1840	2-13-1862
LUCKETT, D. L.		3-29-1795	2-17-1874
NUTTALL, Mary P.	d. of D. L. & Martha F. a. 21 y., 2 m., 28 d.		8- 4-1850
, Sarah G.	w. of D. L. 23rd y		4- 9-1838
PEARCE, Frances A.	84th y.		10-22-1858
, James, Sr.	88th y.		10-27-1857
RODMAN, Sarah E.	w. of Thos.	1-13-1827	
, Thomas		2-24-1791	
ROWLAND, Amanda	w. of Henry	4-18-1810	2-19-1860
SMITH, John		4-13-1802	1-28-1862
, James Clark	s. of Wm. & Lucy	3-10-1837	12-24-1849
, Wm.	a. 77 y.		3-17-1865
, Lucy W.	relict of Wm.	6-10-1799	7-18-1888
THOMASSON, Sarah	consort of Poindexter a. 84 y., 20 d		5-23-1851
, John		2- 7-1829	7-30-1850
, Patsy	mother	3-29-1803	2-22-1884
, Joseph		1837	1901
VALENTINE, William	s. of Rev. B. & Sallie	1-16-1859	6-19-1859

25. Vance Graveyard.
3 m. NW of Port Royal.

Name	Note	Born	Died
CRIM, James		11- 8-1849	4-22-1879
, James	husband	8- 6-1823	2-12-1896
, Louisa		10-30-1823	8-29-1871

DARROUGH, Elizabeth	w. of A.	2-20-1826	5- 9-1862
DAWKING, Thos.	a. 62 y.		12-28-1891
DUNAWAY, Ruah Ann	a. about 86 y.		4-24-1885
, John	a. 56th y.		9-16-1853
EVANS, Annie		1-17-1841	4-24-1908
GAMMON, Sarah C.		11-16-1852	4-26-1905
HAYDEN, Joann	w. of John	2-14-1818	7-30-1880
JONES, W. M.		1- 7-1798	3-14-1856
, James H.		6-12-1854	3- 1-1903
MARSHALL, Martha Ann		4- 3-1846	1-16-1928
RADBOURNE, Clarissa	w. of D. O.	7-21-1840	2-15-1897
SKIDMORE, J. H.		2-28-1839	1- 4-1883
SWITZER, John B.		6-15-1802	8-30-1882
TINGLE, David		10- 7-1865	1- 6-1940
, Lottie	w. of David	8-22-1868	2-14-1940
, W. N.		1855	1951
, Mary C.		4-18-1861	9-22-1924
YOUNG, Artie	husband	1849	
, Duron	w. of A.	1839	1905

26. Turner's Station Public Cemetery.
½ m. SW of Turner's Station.

ADAMS, G. C.	husband	11- 6-1848	
, Melissa	w. of G. C.	12-12-1853	12-12-1926
ADCOCK, Spillsbury	husband	1850	1934
, Mollie Elston	w. of S.	1859	
, Robert Lee	88th FTR, 80th FTR	1919	1946
, Samuel R.		7-25-1895	5- 1-1961
, Margaret L.		5- 6-1867	3-20-1964
, Samuel		1860	1926
ANTILL, Evaline		3- 9-1831	9- 3-1903
BARNETT, Benjamin	husband	1833	1914
, Lucy J.	wife	1842	1889
, John	husband	1860	1932
, Catha	w. of John	1890	1928
, J. Frank	husband	1862	1943
, Betty	wife	1861	1909
BAXTER, Mary A. Johnson	w. of Farmer b. Henry Co., d. Louisville	9-20-1874	10- 6-1906
BOYER, W. T.	husband	6- 4-1831	11- 5-1906
, Mary	wife	3-31-1837	1- 8-1920
CANNON, Alice C.		1880	1963
CHILTON, Wm. Preston	husband	1859	1935
, Mildred Jane	wife	1866	
, John W.	husband	1842	1930
, Victoria	wife	1861	
, Geo. B.	husband	1852	1916
, Elvira C.	wife	1859	1932
, James L.	husband	1868	1943
Laura E.	wife	1875	19--
CLAGETT, James		1831	1921
, Elvessa	w. of J.	1846	1930
CLAGGETT, Smith		1872	1933
, Forest A.	w. of Smith	1884	1964
ELSTON, Lewis Carter	husband	1852	1924
, Bettie Turner	wife	1854	1925
GARRETT, John H.	husband	1864	19--
, Lillie	wife	1868	1942
HARFORD, W. M.	husband	12- 6-1827	11-17-1909
, Elizabeth	wife	2-16-1833	9-29-1923
HAWKINS, Martha Jane		6-20-1839	5-26-1909
HITE, John W.	husband	1874	1916
, Mary C.	wife	9-27-1889	5- 5-1912
JENKINS, W. L.	husband	1843	1922
, Annie L.		1848	1923
JERDEN, W. D.		1868	1926
KNOX, Uley	husband	1897	1962

, Fannie	wife	1896	
McCONNELL, Herbert	husband	1833	1900
, Tabitha	wife	1845	1932
McGARVEY, J. S.			
MILLIGAN, John R.	Ky. S2, USNR WW I	3- 2-1897	7- 2-1964
, Henry	husband	1859	1942
, Nora	wife	1862	1931
NEBLETT, Lizzie Ransdell	w. of J. M.	6-10-1867	11-24-1903
PENDLETON, Lucy A.	w. of R. L.	2-12-1832	2- 1-1893
RANSDELL, Smith C.		1878	1919
SAMUEL, Mary Pendleton		1865	1946
SHADDAY, Albert R.	husband	1867	1926
, Elizabeth F.		1875	
STAPLES, Andrew Jackson	husband	1830	1911
, Anna Mary Vatter	w. of A.	1841	1927
THARP, Richard	Ky. Pvt. US Army WW I	10-19-1895	11- 9-1960
, Jane		1860	1955
R. B.		1860	1927
TURNER, John C.	husband	1857	1939
, Beatrice	wife	1868	1931
, G. R.		1- 9-1853	1-15-1938
, Sally R.		7-17-1856	7-29-1890
, Jennie R.		6- 5-1864	8-28-1899
WAY, Victor F.	husband	1860	1923
, Lena C.	wife	1860	1923
WOODLEY, Dr. James D.		1868	1944
, Lillian B.	w. of Dr. J. D.	1885	1959

27. Port Royal Baptist Church Graveyard.
West edge of Port Royal.

ADCOCK, J. A.		1867	1937
, Ludie	w. of J. A.	1873	1933
BARNETT, George		5-20-1880	10- 2-1959
, Mebel	w. of Geo.	3-31-1880	
BATTS, Joe B.	husband	1858	1916
, Jane Rife	w. of J. B.	1864	1934
, Joel M.		1855	1927
, Alice	w. of J. M.	1856	1933
BERRY, Lucinda		1827	1916
, James H.		1850	1925
, John J.		1824	1893
BEVARLY, Henry Clay		8- 6-1846	12-21-1914
, Nannie K.	w. of H. C.	1855	1944
BOULWARE, Mattie A.	w. of S. O.	4-10-1847	3-26-1876
, Isaac Newton	w. of L. F. & C. B.	1851	1869
, L. F.	husband	6- 9-1818	1-18-1875
, Corallae	w. of L. F.	10-30-1828	10-22-1880
, Linna		5-22-1874	10-18-1893
CARTER, J. O. A.	Co. L, 12th US Inf.	8- 1-1877	1- 1-1900
, T. M.		1845	1937
, Lewis	w. of T. M.	1847	
CHILTON, Malisia E.		10- 9-1866	5-12-1883
, Lucy L.	d. of G. G. & F. B.	7-18-1875	2-26-1876
, Louis W.		5-19-1862	1-23-1949
, Mattie E.		7- 4-1865	2-26-1916
, Lucy E.		1-14-1839	10-16-1914
, Millie Ann	w. of Wm.	5-26-1830	3-11-1915
, John F.	h. of F. B.	1851	1927
, Florence B.	w. of J. F.	10-16-1850	9-16-1890
COBLIN, Eliza Jane	w. of J.	11-25-1816	3-26-1877
, Sarah	w. of J. P.	6-13-1847	1- 2-1876
CORLEY, Mary D.		1846	1926
CRIM, Nancy E.	w. of James	5-13-1835	1-20-1902
DARROUGH, J. H.		12-15-1847	12-28-1918
, Sallie	w. of J. H.	8-26-1847	2-15-1920
DUNAWAY, John		1850	1935
, Rettie	w. of J.	1852	1935
, Samuel		8- 4-1843	7-12-1937
, Ella	w. of Sam	10-25-1856	4-29-1851

ELLIS, J. B.	husband	2-22-1799	9-20-1878
, Hannah	w. of J. B.		11-12-1878
	a. 84 y.		
FOWLER, Rev. John M.		9-30-1858	7-16-1923
, Lucy Chilton	w. of J. M.	6- 1-1860	8-10-1947
HANKS, T.	husband	2-27-1822	1- 6-1898
, Sallie E.	w. of Thos.	11- 9-1851	8-16-1890
HARRIS, Edmund J.	husband		8-29-1840
	a. 50 y.		
, Lucy	a. 47 y.		8-28-1840
HAWKINS, G. W.		2-22-1848	8- 2-1915
, Matilda	w. of J. N.	1-24-1815	3-21-1898
HUMSTON, Amos D.	husband	1850	1891
Martha F.	wife	1856	1936
, James O.		1874	1924
JOHNSON, Dr. Calvin R.		1854	1932
, Lucy B.	w. of Dr. C. R.	1854	1936
JONES, Mary E.	d. of A. J. & M.	3-30-1841	8-15-1870
, Jennie M.	w. of T. M.	3-24-1833	2-14-1873
KITSON, Lucy	w. of A. P.	12-30-1865	3- 2-1885
LANDERS, H. G.	husband	9- 6-1863	12-29-1916
, Mollie	wife	10-25-1870	
MATTICK, Johnie	s. of H. & J. L.	3-26-1860	7-26-1874
MINOR, Norvin R.	s. of Geo. & Mary P.	1872	1873
, Mary	w. of G. C.	2-13-1839	4-12-1876
, V. H.	husband	2- 4-1862	4- 2-1895
, Mildred	w. of V. H.	10-15-1835	11- 6-1902
PENISTON, A.M.		7- 7-1837	10-23-1907
, M. D.	w. of A. M.	7-22-1842	12- 9-1918
PERRY, Jemima	w. of B. H.	5-22-1779	7-16-1831
	a. 55 y., 2 m., 6 d		
, B. H., Jr.		9-19-1813	3- 3-1885
, Greenup		6- 5-1812	12-22-1885
, Lucy		5-19-1816	2- 7-1902
, John Allen		9-18-1818	7-25-1839
, Sallie		6-14-1815	6-19-1872
, B. H.	husband	1-12-1777	12-24-1856
, Mary		10-18-1805	3- 8-1837
, Washington		4-22-1803	1-12-1875
, Milton		1- 8-1838	3- 1-1913
, Frances	w. of M.	3-24-1843	5-13-1923
, Harriet		12-29-1839	2- 3-1907
, T. J.		1808	1889
, Sarah	w. of T. J.	11-24-1816	9-16-1909
, Martha		5-15-1813	1-24-1893
, Elige R.		1841	1909
POLLARD, William	husband	6- 1-1811	9- 7-1869
, Elizabeth	w. of Wm.	1-21-1818	7-26-1891
POWELL, Susan C.	w. of E. K.	11- 9-1837	11-28-1878
, Elisha K.		2-19-1833	2-10-1878
RANKLEY, Frank, Sr.	husband	10- 1-1805	12- 9-1900
, Mary	w. of Frank	6- 8-1819	11-18-1889
RICKETS, Susan G.		1834	1934
SHELTON,	s. of H. & M. J.	8-31-1861	11- 3-1874
SMITH, Kirby		3- 4-1863	7- 5-1897
THOMAS, Lucy E.	w. of N. L.	8-23-1842	4- 9-1870
TINGLE, Elisha	husband	11- 8-1819	3-19-1900
, J. Binia	w. of E.	8-28-1819	2-24-1900
, Levi		9-17-1836	2- 4-1926
, Mary E.	w. of Levi	1- 5-1841	12-15-1909
TIPTON, Virginia Massie		1849	1921
WILSON, R. S.	husband	5-20-1832	3- 5-1914
, Mary A.	w. of R. S.	3-24-1851	9- 6-1927

28. Antill Graveyard.
On Port Royal Road, 3 m. NW of New Castle

ANTILL, Thomas		3-16-1816	1-21-1887
, Keziah	w. of Thos.	3-24-1819	3-16-1864

Name	Note	Born	Died
, John		5-12-1790	8- 5-1860
, Henry		4-12-1796	3-28-1854
, Elleanora	w. of Jacob	7-30-1846	8- 4-1875
BETHWICK, Mountair	a. 24		5-26-1844
BODKIN, Polly	w. of Chas.		
BOYER, John L.		11- 9-1821	12- 9-1894
CHANDLER, Eva Z.	w. of F.	3-13-1863	5- 6-1889
SHUCK, Wina F.		5-22-1806	1-27-1861

29. Eminence Public Cemetery.
S. edge of Eminence. (* denotes burial in Odd Fellows' Section).

Name	Note	Born	Died
*ADAMS, Patience		5-17-1804	8- 6-1890
* , John B.		1831	1913
*ANDERSON, J. R.		10-13-1829	1-28-1907
*BARNETT, William		1833	1904
* , James W.		1862	1938
* , Mary Ditto		1873	1958
BATTS, James H.	b. on Guam Island	1923	1944
, John W.		1860	1943
, Carrie	w. of J. W.	1864	1915
BELL, Maurice	M. D.	1871	1964
, Pearl C.	w. of M.	1879	1955
*BERRY, T. A.		10-15-1831	8- 1-1904
*BLACKABY, Thomas		1835	1928
*BLAKEMORE, James Marcus		10- 3-1842	2-12-1911
* , Elizabeth Armstrong	w. of J. M.	8-14-1844	8-12-1908
*BOHANNAN, Charles Richard		1891	1964
* , Louise Peterson	w. of C. R.		
* , Joshua		11-25-1869	3-21-1935
* , Alice C.	w. of J.	7-27-1868	3-27-1942
*BOSHARDT,	father	1828	1906
*	mother	1841	1912
*BOULWARE, Sallie Turk	w. of R. H. m. 11-12-1835	11- 4-1815	1-19-1885
* , (Three infant graves)			
* , Lucy J.	w. of N. C.	11-28-1849	7- 4-1881
* , Nathan C.		1845	1918
* , Maurice Donaldson		1888	1907
* , Stephen D.		1864	1938
* , Mary Ann	w. of S. D.	1864	1931
* , James R.		8-14-1836	4- 4-1878
BREWER, J. A.		12- 9-1832	3-18-1887
, Mattie F.	w. of J. A.	2- 2-1861	7- 5-1873
*BRIGHT, Newton		1876	1963
* , Maye Maddox	w. of Newton	1874	1958
* , Newton		10-23-1829	
* , Dorcas Helm		8-10-1834	3-17-1910
* , Jeptha		1793	1870
* , Elizabeth Emma	w. of J.	1799	1873
* , Jeptha		1862	1929
* , Teresa Fitzgerald		1865	1940
*BURTON, Ernest Linwood		1878	1961
CALDWELL, Kate B.		1873	1938
CALLAWAY, Mary Jane		11-14-1829	1-16-1901
, Samuel H.		6- 4-1825	12- 9-1899
* , James		4- 3-1803	1- 1-1878
* , Cindarilla			
* , Parham		1818	1902
* , America R. Yount	w. of P.	1824	1875
* , Wm. C.		12- 9-1822	1-27-1898
* , Mary J.	w. of W. C.	12-27-1829	11- 4-1900
* , John Samuel		1836	1896
* , F. Cordelia		1843	1922
* , Samuel		1807	1853
* , Martha Durrett		1815	1887
* , Elizabeth Todd		1833	1881
* , James M.		10- 1-1834	1-26-1877

*CAMPBELL, Dr. J. P.		5- 1-1838	12-18-1869
*CARTER, Jessie		1851	1938
*CLUB, Socrates		1849	1917
* , Nannie	w. of Socrates	1861	1947
*CLUBB, William E.		1837	1927
* , Mary L.	w. of W. E.	1846	1925
*COLEMAN, Martha Callaway		1838	1907
CORBIN, John S.		1842	1932
, Marium E.		1845	1919
*CRABB, J. M.		1833	1915
* , Nancy B.		1-27-1802	5- 9-1888
* , S. D.	in 69th y.		11- 7-1870
* , James G., III		1925	1933
* , F. R.		1858	1920
* , A. C.		1-25-1817	7- 6-1876
* , Lou R.		1834	1921
*CRAWFORD, Moses H.		1825	1872
* , Fannie G.	w. of Moses	1835	1913
*CURL, A. D.		1859	1930
DAWSON, E. S.		12-17-1813	2-13-1896
, L. A.	w. of E. S.	5-19-1820	11-20-1901
DEMAREE, Clarence		1867	1955
, Catherine	w. of Clarence	1870	1935
DICKEN, E. H.		1812	1888
*DITTO, Lowe W.		1868	1907
* , William		1865	1915
* , E. F.		1840	1919
* , Meranda Kephart		1847	1924
*DOWNS, James M.		1864	1920
* , Sallie B.	w. of James M.	1865	1946
*DRANE, J. W.		1862	1925
* , Henry H.		1865	1953
* , Lewis Tillet		1866	1923
* , Mary Miller	w. of L. T.	1872	1953
* , Stephen			
* , Prissilla	w. of Stephen		
* , J. H.		3-31-1805	10-23-1892
* , Nancy	w. of J. H.	3-11-1801	1-21-1883
* , P. S.		1-11-1765	11-14-1831
*DUERSON, B. W.		1809	6- 8-1873
DUNNAVENT, Jonathon		1-29-1823	9-23-1894
ELLIS, Lewis S.		1841	1920
, Adelia		1851	1921
* , Henry C.		2-21-1815	5-26-1877
* , Margaret J.	w. of H. C.	12- 9-1827	10-28-1853
*FALLIS, Victor		1861	1915
* , Ray Thompson		1866	1949
FISHER, Thomas C.		3- 1-1833	7-16-1897
*FLEMING, Robert T.		1862	1948
* , Ella K.	w. of R. T.	1866	1931
*FUQUA, John S.		1829	1911
* , Nannie J.		1840	1906
* , J. R.	b. in Mexico	1863	1915
* , Geo. Coffer		1866	1953
*GIBSON, Mary H.	w. of J. S. d. of J. B. & F. Roberts	12-23-1796	4- 6-1871
GILTNER, William Henry		1871	1937
, Margaret Head		1876	1961
* , W. S.		5-18-1827	12-15-1921
* , Lizzie Raines	w. of W. S.	2- 3-1838	6- 8-1894
*GREENE, Bobby Ann		1925	1928
*GUTHRIE, John S.		1860	1924
* , Sallie Rickets	w. of J. S.	1850	1918
*HANNA, Charles Morton		1848	1910
* , Mattie Allen	w. of C. M.	1858	1939
* , C. Morton		1896	1964
HARDESTY, Jacob		2- 1-1816	6- 5-1897
, Dianah M.	w. of J.	1-30-1820	6-10-1902
HELM, W. S.		5- 6-1806	3- 4-1885
Joseph A.		1839	1886

Name	Relation	Born	Died
Mary Helen	w. of J. A.	1842	1918
Ann		1816	1898
HERNDON, J. C.		1856	1917
, Lou Coleman		8-31-1850	12- 4-1936
*HIEATT, Meredith P.		1819	1886
* , Sarah F.		1836	1905
HINKLE, John S.		1845	1917
, Matilda T.	w. of J. S.	1851	1919
HOCKER, Jesse C.		8-18-1857	1-19-1905
HORNSBY, Joseph W.		12- 8-1838	2- 3-1918
, Jennie C.		5-28-1853	8-11-1932
IRELAND, J. Crit		8- 5-1835	8-27-1893
*JACOBY, George A.		1867	1904
* , Sarah E.		1898	1900
JENKINS, William B.		1865	1947
, John L.		7- 8-1809	5- 6-1884
, W. Susana		2-19-1825	6-12-1893
KALUSY, Lizzie Devore		1887	1960
*KELLEY, R. J. Smith	w. of G.	1815	1893
* , Griffin		1-25-1810	11- 1-1887
KERLIN, John		1843	1922
*KLEISER, John R.		1855	1931
* , Emlie Roy	w. of J. R.	1857	1948
* , Robert Henry		1829	1868
* , Susan Yates	w. of R. H.	1831	1912
* , John		10- 8-1798	12-28-1877
* , Matilda Bird	w. of John	3- 5-1808	5- 8-1887
KNIGHT, Emma	w. of Frank	8- 9-1860	3-23-1888
*LACY, Charles A.		1858	1898
LONG, Talmadge		1883	1941
, Effie A.	w. of T.	1885	1959
McELWAIN, Thos. J.		1847	1931
, Ada Lee	w. of T. J.	1860	1945
, Mrs. Cordelia Ann	w. of John	9-15-1814	8-23-1896
* , Henry		6-26-1817	2-26-1890
* , Margaret A.	d. of Geo. & Mary Penn w. of Henry	9- 7-1819	6- 3-1871
* , Samuel		7-16-1807	2-12-1887
* , Harriett	w. of Samuel	2- 5-1812	
* , W. H.		1838	1894
* , Elizabeth Work	w. of W. H.	1843	1920
* , James Sanders		1829	1905
* , Alice Stoddard	w. of J. S.	1847	1932
*McROBERTS, John		11-28-1809	12-29-1892
* , Nancy	w. of John	11-29-1809	6-13-1885
* , Elijah		1-11-1812	2- 3-1865
MADDOX, Emily		2-14-1814	7-17-1853
, Loulie M.	w. of J. H.	6- 1-1852	3- 7-1878
, Evelyn		1842	1916
, David Sanford		11- 7-1820	9-26-1876
, Henry		2-25-1813	7-15-1905
, Mary Stone	w. of Henry	6- 5-1821	9-12-1871
MAGRUDER, Josiah		12- 8-1822	7- 3-1901
*MASON, W. J.		1810	1888
* , Amanda	w. of W. J.	1815	1886
*MELONE, Beverly P.		1870	1911
*MIDDLETON, Thomas Preston		5-14-1868	6- 4-1946
* , Eddie Gaines		5- 1-1866	2-15-1956
MOORE, James Harvey		8-20-1824	9-30-1898
, Sarah E.	w. of J. H.	9-25-1831	1-20-1871
*MOSS, C. W.		1854	1916
* , F. O.	w. of C. W.	1855	
* , John Ray		5-18-1826	5-31-1893
* , Emeline	w. of J. R.	9-23-1827	9-13-1877
NUTTALL, Thoughtless		8-25-1873	4-13-1937
*O'BANNON, James		1821	1908
* , Susan F.		1835	1923
POLLARD, John F.		1853	1939
*PORTER, D. N.		1-17-1816	1-29-1903
*PRYOR, Mary McElwain	w. of Jack	7-10-1843	3-24-1888

*PURYEAR, C. A.			1850	1929
*REES, Abram			5-10-1806	11-10-1875
* , Nancy J.	w. of Abram		8-22-1816	12-13-1889
* , Joseph T.			11-12-1850	10-29-1881
* , J. J.			1835	1896
* , R. C.			1837	1923
*RICHARDSON, W. L.			1862	1939
* , Wingfield			1857	1922
*ROBERTS, Prentice T.			1899	1942
*ROBERTSON, Eugene Beverly			10-18-1866	2-10-1957
*ROWLAND, George J.			1-14-1811	6- 4-1870
* , Harriett	w. of G. J.		2-17-1832	7-27-1900
*RUNYON, Malitha			1832	1929
*SCOTT, Levi H.			1827	1908
* , Louisa M.			1835	1906
*SEWELL, J. H.			1866	1922
* , Margaret	w. of J. H.		3-16-1868	5- 3-1905
*SLOAN, Edmund Lewis			9-23-1852	3- 5-1937
SNOOK, W. B.			1860	1918
, Lucy Flood			1872	1942
STARK, Julia Foote			1844	1921
, Wm. Edward			1836	1898
*STRAUGHAN, J. L.			4-19-1829	12- 1-1901
*THOMAS, Scott B.			1898	1929
* , Harry C.			1895	1944
* , Edwin B.			1870	1942
* , Ella Brewer			1875	1926
* , Oswald			9-10-1769	8-12-1855
* , Mary	w. of Oswald		3-10-1775	5-30-1854
* , James William	husband		1838	1919
* , Mary Wilson	wife		7-29-1844	8-11-1928
* , John			11-28-1807	1-23-1843
* , Preston			11-29-1811	11- 3-1869
* , Joseph			7- 2-1849	9-26-1875
, James Preston			1870	1937
, Oswald	husband		1840	1909
* , Annie L.	w. of Oswald		4- 1-1847	11-15-1882
THORNE, Gov. W. P.				
, Anna D.				
, W. K.	father			
, Mary M.	w. of W. K.	mother		
*TINSLEY, Richard L.			8- 8-1824	1- 2-1903
* , Elizabeth G.	w. of R. L.		3-21-1833	10-20-1903
THORNTON, Nellie B.			1879	1940
TODD, John			8-24-1806	3- 6-1873
*UNDERWOOD, Dr. I. M.			2- 6-1815	4-20-1871
* , Matilda	w. of Dr. I. M.			
WAIDE, Minnie			1869	1875
WAUGH, Bernice T.			1873	1924
*WILSON, Lilla P.			1854	1855
* , Wm. B.			1820	1906
* , Elizabeth O.			1821	1864
* , Amanda Crocket			1851	1909
*WOODS, Ahijah			8-16-1804	2-11-1880
* , Nancy	consort of A.		5- 5-1804	10-16-1870
*YAGER, Annie Wright			1869	1960
*YEAGER, Mary Rees			6-12-1853	10-27-1909

(Only oldest graves taken).

30. Cemetery Hill Church of Christ.
Highway 22, 2 m. SW of Gratz.

BATES, Z. T.		11- 9-1835	7-23-1897
, Nancy	w. of Zach	4- 2-1842	6-14-1873
HOSKIN, Rubie (Rube)		4- 6-1871	
, Cora	w. of R.	2-12-1879	
PRICE, Louella	w. of Harlan	1-13-1863	1-14-1893

ROBERTS, Annie	w. of N.	8-17-1820	6-19-1892
, Frances Ellen	w. of J. N.	9- 8-1848	5-22-1873
, John B.		3- 7-1812	8-17-1869
, Elizabeth	w. of J. B.	2- 5-1819	9- 8-1906
SANDERS, Fannie S.	w. of David	1859	1883

(Additional graves not listed).

31. Bevarly Cemetery.
S bank of Ky. River, halfway between Gratz and Lockport.

BEVARLY, Stephen		5-15-1826	6- 8-1889
, A. H.		1863	1917
, Nannie	w. of A. H.	6-24-1865	7-14-1893
DUNCAN, Robert A.		12- 7-1837	
McALISTER, Ewing		7- 6-1807	6-16-1893
, Matilda	w. of Ewing 77th y		12-20-1887
, Michael		5-24-1826	10-16-1880
RANKINS, Rebecca	w. of Sept.	5-13-1800	3-22-1872
SHAW, Elijah		11-27-1841	1-23-1904
, Nancy B.	w. of Elijah	8-15-1844	

32. Point Pleasant Cemetery.
2 m. W of Bethlehem.

BEUTEL, Thos. F.		1861	1919
, Rebecca		1869	1935
BRYANT, W. B.		1854	1918
, F.	w. of W. B.	1862	
HALL, John T.		1839	1926
, Lucinda	w. of J. T.	1842	1883
HOLLEY, Wm.		1-19-1799	8-31-1870
, Mary	w. of Wm.	5- 8-1802	10- 2-1871
KELLY, Elizabeth Benson	b. Sheffield, England	6-18-1818	11-20-1892
	husband b. Isle of Man	1- 2-1809	9-26-1876
PORTER, Harriett, B.	w. of Phil T.	9-11-1835	3-29-1880

33. 3 m. W of New Castle on Fallen Timber Road.
Newton Jeffries, Jr., owner.

BRENT, Elizabeth Duncan	1st w. of J. L.	1- 8-1816	6- 7-1843

34. Scobee Graveyard, W. P. Stivers, owner.
3 m. W of New Castle on Fallen Timber Road

BARNHILL, Kate	w. of James W. a. 21 y., 5 m., 9 d.		8-19-1872
, Mary M.	d. of J. W. & K. a. 6 m.		1872
BICKNELL, C. M.		10- 1-1838	12-10-1885
McDONALD, Jac W.		6-20-1815	1- 9-1895
, Letitia	w. of J. W.	12-18-1816	8-24-1870
MASSIE, Jessie		3-27-1812	12-22-1872
, Frederica	w. of Jessie	9-14-1820	10- 4-1872
, Bettie	d. of J. & F.	11-14-1843	5-10-1870
SCOBEE, Joseph Simpson	s. of Christee & Polly	6-14-1843	6- 5-1890
, Hannah		9-18-1828	12-26-1900
, Robert W.		5- 9-1838	4-15-1900
, Virgil Warren	s. of J. C. & Jennie	12-12-1896	12- -1896
, Mary C.		1847	1863
, Stephen, Sr.	a. 96 y., 11 m., 19 d.	1- 7-1773	12-26-1866
, Hannah	w. of Stephen	3- 5-1775	7-14-1855
SPENCER, James W.		11-24-1841	1-21-1877
Lizzie H.	d. of J. W. & M. J.	7-21-1874	8-24-1876
TANNER, Rev. Archelaus	Episcopal Methodist preacher b. Bourt----, d. Henry Co.	4-20-1818	4-19-1850

35. Beasley Cemetery.
3 m. W of New Castle on New Castle-Sulphur Road.

BEASLEY, Elizabeth	w. of H.	9-20-1777	11-28-1858

36. Walker Graveyard.
4 m. E of Sulphur on New Castle Road.

SHOUSE, Sally	w. of J. H.	12-12-1806	11-17-1852
, "Little Sammie"	s. of R. L. & M. J.	10- 6-1864	4-11-1866

37. Campbellsville Primitive Baptist Church Graveyard.
N end of Campbellsburg.

ASHBROOK, R. M.		4- 9-1852	4-11-1895
, Mary E.		3- 4-1859	2-11-1936
BROWN, Sarah	w. of James	1-17-1811	7-23-1880
, James			
CHANDLER, Frank Y.		1860	1933
Sarah Adaline	his w.	1869	1952
CHILTON, James F.		1851	1934
, Cassie	w. of J. F.	6-15-1850	3-22-1887
, Wm. S.		1877	1966
, Gerty P.		1878	1965
CRAWFORD, Christopher H.		11-17-1818	3-29-1895
GIVIDEN, Ollie	w. of John E.	5-23-1864	5-18-1892
HAYDEN, Edward		1-18-1807	9- 1-1869
HUMSTON, W. T.		1840	1917
, Alberta M.		1856	1886
, Mary E.	w. of W. A.	4- 5-1844	5-10-1875
JEWELL, N. R.		1855	1906
JOHNSTON, Margaret E.	w. of F. H.	12-16-1839	10-11-1868
JONES, Wm.		3-11-1787	5-25-1846
, Mary A.	wife	4- 4-1797	3-17-1884
KELLY, James		1813	1896
, Polly		1813	1896
, Wm.		1850	1926
KNIGHT, Elder John		8-18-1793	9-20-1873
PYLES, Emma D.	w. of Marion	12-19-1852	3-22-1881
, Abraham		4-12-1805	11-18-1881
, Maria	w. of T. J.	11- 3-1803	7-26-1885
, Thomas		9- 2-1808	9- 2-1902
RINGO, Sarah	w. of Geo., Sr.	5- 7-1801	12-18-1867
, George		2-22-1800	4-14-1881
SAMS, W. C.		1-18-1813	6-15-1900
, Lucinda	w. of W. C.	5- 8-1817	4-25-1877
VORIES, Elizabeth	w. of James	10- -1799	12-10-1863
, James		6-22-1799	8-21-1881
, Francis		5- 3-1795	4-24-1882

38. Hwy. 155, 2 m. E of Sulphur, Mrs. Lyda Gividen, owner.

MARTIN, Micajah		9-11-1805	7-23-1852
, Elizabeth		3- 1-1813	11-29-1877

39. Estes-McClellan place, Billy McClellan, owner.
End of Martini Lane.

ESTES, W. M.		3- 4-1819	2- 8-1901

40. Old Martini Farm Graveyard, Kenny Melvin, owner.
Martini Lane ½ m. S of Hwy. 421.

STATEN, John Thomas	s. of James & Mary	12-13-1848	10-21-1867

, Elizabeth	w. of Joseph	1-27-1819	2-15-1872
, Joseph		10-18-1811	12-18-1859

41. Drennon Church Graveyard.

BISHOP, George W.		1841	1889
CRAWFORD, R. B.		1861	1944
, Mary	his wife	1864	
COOK, Norbourne B.		1786	1866
DYKE, J. A. W.		1847	1926
, Nann	his wife	1847	
ERWIN, E. Tandy		1859	1929
, Judith L.	his wife	1-15-1861	
FITZGERALD, Samuel		1864	1910
, Mary Belle		1868	1919
HENDERSON, Leonard		1883	1972
, Allie J.	his wife	1887	1963
, W. H.		1822	1901
HULETT, J. W.		1858	1928
JONES, W. O.		1864	1936
, Laura	his wife	1869	1931
, Jesse		1847	1891
, Samuel		1849	1918
, Nancy	his wife	1854	1927
KALUSY, Andrew		1811	1858
LOUDEN, Cordelia Mahorney		1862	1947
MAHONEY, Mary E.	wife	1864	1938
, John A.	husband	1864	1942
MAHORNEY, J. W.		1858	1925
, Eliza	his wife	1859	1939
, Lark		1852	
, Sally	his wife	1858	1921
MERTZ, Joseph		1865	1873
QUICKERT, Antony		9- 5-1814	7- 4-1900
TINGLE, Wm. J.		1869	1942
, Susie E.	his wife	1887	19--

42. Hwy. 421, W end of Campbellsburg.

SCOTT, Lucy Anne	w. of Chilton a. 23 y., 2 m., 8 d.		10-22-1843

43. Singleton Farm.
1 m. S of Lacie, KY.

BISHOP, Sarah		1810	10- -1836
CRAVENS, Elizabeth	w. of A.	6-29-1791	1-16-1867
McCRACKEN, William	Senator	1-15-1778	10-26-1860
, William	s. of Wm. & Jane	8- 6-1804	4- 4-1826
, Jane	w. of Wm.	2-22-1781	6-16-1867

44. 2 m. NE of Turner's Station on Port Royal-Turner's Station Road.

CHILTON, H. S.		12-29-1826	8-20-1904
, Susan	w. of H. S.	7-11-1828	
, George		1801	1859
, Charles F.		1815	1855
, Lucinda	w. of W. H.	6-10-1843	7-17-1878
MOREHEAD, Mariah	w. of G. Chilton & Enoch Morehead	1807	1890
RANSDELL, B. F.		6-20-1820	12- 1-1880
	1st w. of B. F.	5- 5-1820	3- 9-1846
, Martha	2nd w. of B. F.	1825	1862
, Isabel	3rd w. of B. F.	1835	1894

45. Quinley-Jackson Graveyard.
2 m. NW of Turner's Station, middle of Monfort Lane.

CHILTON, Emily E.	d. of J. W. & E.	1874	1886
JACKSON, Emma		1859	1899
QUINLEY, Mary M.	w. of T. J.	7- 2-1849	3- 9-1870

46. Bryant Graveyard, Ralph Tindall, owner.
1 m. S of Campbellsburg on Hillsboro Road.

BRYANT, Infant of T. C. & L.		1880	1881
, Infant of T. C. & L.		1878	1883

47. Union Baptist Churchyard.
4 m. E of Defoe and 3 m. N of Hwy. 421.

ADAMS, Arthur		1881	1921
, Pearl	w.	1887	1944
BAKER, Alice	w. of James A.	4- 9-1856	10-25-1878
BOHANAN, Eliza	w. of Thos.	1856	1893
, Nancy		1800	1891
CARTER, Fannie		1860	1937
CHADWELL, Mary J. Black	w. of James	1851	1881
CURTIS, Mary B.	w. of John	1855	1888
ETHRINGTON, Susan M.	w. of J. E.	1864	1888
HARLOWE, Sterling		2-19-1836	12-24-1868
HUDSON, Angeline	a. 62 y.		1879
HUGHES, M. C.	a. 63 y.		1895
JOHNSON, Weldon		1852	1880
MAYBERRY, B. F.		1857	1945
MILLER, W. B.		1868	1934
, Jane	wife	1876	
NEAL, Irvin		1889	1890
, Geo. W.		1837	1893
ROBERTS, Mary J.		1858	1917
, Susan	w. of Emanuel	1829	1891
, James		1800	1893
, Vinia	w. of J. E.	1876	1897
, Dudley	s. of James & Mary	1840	1872
, Mary	w. of J.	3-11-1816	3-26-1891
STIVERS. Ida	w. of Willie	1869	1889

48. Coppersmith Graveyard.
Hwy. 561, 2 m. N of Campbellsburg.

COPPERSMITH, Jacob			
, Elizabeth	w. of Wm.	1830	1879
, Wm.		1824	1890
EDDINS, Sarah E.		8- 2-1887	4- 2-1969
HOPKINS, Frank		1881	1920
KUPPERSMITH, L. V. Tovikar	w. of W.		
THOMPSON, Lee T.	11 inf., 5 div. WW II	8- 2-1921	8- 2-1944
, Samuel F.		1898	1970
, Ethel	wife	1906	1970

49. Woodfill Graveyard.
Bethlehem, behind Bethlehem Methodist Church.

WOODFILL, John L.		9-25-1809	2-25-1888
, Jane	w. of J. L.	2-13-1812	1-30-1883
, John	a. 87 y., 1 m., 7 d.		3- 5-1866
, J. R.		1836	1865

50. Sewell-Adams Graveyard.
Behind Bethlehem Methodist Church, Bethlehem.

ADAMS, W. M.	s. of J. & S.	1841	1863
SEWELL, Mary C.	w. of L. W.	7-28-1848	7-28-1901
----		1833	1879

51. Sewell Graveyard.
2 m. N of Bethlehem.

JESSE, Cynthia	w. of J. W.	7- 2-1841	12-24-1915
, James W.		5- 9-1837	7-18-1909
SEWELL, Annie	w. of J. B. a. 24 y.		8- 7-1893
, A. M.		10-29-1847	8-25-1912
, Elizabeth	w. of Sanford		
, Sanford	a. 59 y., 2 m., 24 d.		3-23-1893
, Hattie	w. of L. W.	7-13-1840	6-18-1887
, Joseph		10-16-1793	11- 5-1882
, Catherine	w. of Joseph	6-17-1785	9- 5-1879

52. Carr Graveyard.
3 m. N of Franklinton.

CARR, Infant	s. of W. M. & C. A.	1867	1867
, Cynthia	w. of W. M.	11- 6-1839	5-18-1870
, Isabel		1827	1902
, D. H.		1824	1904
, J. H.		1832	1916
Wm. N.		12-24-1834	11-24-1878

53. Mt. Gilead.

CARR, N. B.		1824	1881
GAINS, Bernard		3-12-1797	8-16-1886
GALBRAITH, Wm.		1797	1853
JONES, Edna B.	w. of J.	1855	1876
LOUDEN, Allen		1823	1881
, John		5-19-1790	2-23-1865
McGREW, Emily		1845	1928
SUTTON, Wm.		2-20-1804	11- 9-1884
, Mahala	w. of Wm.	9-26-1811	
YOUNG, Rev. J. L.		1818	1900

54. Pollard Home, Kenneth Cox, owner.

BAKER, Isaac	a. 50		8-18-1833
, Lettie	w. of Isaa a. 75 y., 8 m		1859
, Elijah		10-18-1817	1860
, Sam W.		1825	1840
POLLARD, Mariam Parmer	w. of E. B.	1841	1861
, Mary Ann		1833	
, Nicholas S.		3-28-1837	5- 9-1860
, Elijah		12-22-1770	7-20-1823
, Nancy	consort of Elijah	1-10-177-	1851
, Nancy	w. of Hamlet	1819	1862
, J. I.		1808	1892

55. Knight-Guthrie-O'Bannon Graveyard.

ADAMS, David Esq.		1785	
DODD, Catherine	d. of James & Eliz. 50th y.		9-29-1849

Name	Notes	Born	Died
, Elizabeth	consort of James 81st y		1785
, James	a. 75 y., 3 m., 19 d.		9- 9-1833
GRIGSBY, Lewis		1843	1865
GUTHRIE, Robt.			2-19-1842
, Archibald	a. 27 y.		1830
KNIGHT, John A.	s. of Jeremiah & Nancy a. 7 m.		1838
, Nancy	w. of Jeremiah a. 39 y., 4 m.		1-17-1849
LONG, Mary			1835
O'BANNON, Harvenia	consort of C. a. 27 y., 10 m., 21 d.		5-12-1837
OWEN, Sarah		8-12-1796	6-10-1853
SMITH, Martha Ann	d. of James & Hannah a. 2 y.		9- 3-1831
, Robert	82nd y.		1840
, Nicholas	a. 9 y., 4 m.		6-18-1835
STURGEON, Samuel	a. 70 y.		1828
TAYLOR, Cranston	64th y.		4-15-1830
, Charlotte	consort of Cranston 64th y.		11-19-1833
TODD, Wm. P.	s. of James & Mary a. 4 y., 11 m.		9-25-1831

56. Grub Ridge Christian Church.
Bethlehem and Bestville Road, 6 m. E of Bethlehem

Name	Notes	Born	Died
AYNES, David P.		6-15-1859	10-15-1922
, Pernelle T.		1860	1941

HENRY COUNTY CEMETERIES [KENTUCKY]

Part II

by
Robert Foster Johnson

HENRY COUNTY CEMETERIES: PART II

By Robert Foster Johnson*

56. Grub Ridge Christian Church.
Bethlehem and Bestville Road, 6 m. E of Bethlehem.

Name	Note	Born	Died
ADAMS, Oris		8-21-1875	9-11-1918
AYNES, David P.		6-15-1859	10-15-1922
, Pernelle T.		1860	1941
BAILEY, Nell		1883	1952
, Alex		1883	1952
, Mary T.	mother	1900	1929
BANTA, Mary E.		1855	1937
, Daniel F.		1850	1929
, Delvin		1884	1919
, Cassie D.		1888	1919
BELIE, Sterling		1889	1956
BENNETT, Mary E.		10-22-1865	6- 8-1934
BLACK, G. B.		1860	1925
, Rebecca	w. of G. B.	1859	1939
BLACKABY, H.		4-11-1877	
, Lucy	w. of H.	4-23-1879	7-17-1931
, John		1837	1921
, Rebecca	w. of John	1837	1920
BRAMBLETT, Lucy		9-10-1860	1-28-1928
, R. J.		10-20-1862	7-12-1915
BROWN, E. G.		1878	1914
CHANDLER, Perry		1879	1939
CHISHOLM, William		5-16-1850	1-31-1933
, Maggie	w. of Wm.	4-10-1867	2-10-1946
, Charles		1878	1965
, Lucy Downey	w. of Chas.	1888	1964
, Druzella		5-22-1851	4-15-1919
, E. C.		12- 2-1895	
, Rosa E.	w. of E. C.	9-23-1896	1-13-1927
, Ernest	WW I	1895	1962
, John W.		6- 9-1915	12- 3-1937
, J. C.		2-15-1849	12- 2-1922
CLARK, Lizzie S.		6-14-1854	11-14-1937
CLEMENTS, Clarence		1892	1967
, Ethel		1892	
COX, - - -		1-14-1908	11-30-1923
CRAWFORD, Sallie		8-19-1884	6-12-1946
DEARINGER, Harvey		5-25-1860	11- 4-1900
, Lucy		4-23-1862	4-15-1918
DOWNEY, David		1-11-1887	5-18-1964
, Dow		1860	1918
, Fronia	w. of Dow	1864	1928
, Eddie		1893	1918
, Martha Jane		3-19-1869	4-27-1948
, Wesley D.		12- 5-1872	1-27-1919
, C. W.		5- 3-1840	
, Elizabeth	w. of C. W.	6-30-1842	10- 3-1918
, Richard		1879	1954
ETHINGTON, M. S.		4-19-1937	6- 1-1939
FLACK, James J.		1853	1888
, Margaret J.		8-10-1859	12-20-1945
FLOOD, Daisy T.	w. of Onie	2- 5-1898	7-17-1915
HALL, Z. T.		4- 2-1847	5-16-1895
, Martin		1886	1959
, Rena Sanders	w. of Martin	1886	
, G. T.		1853	1930
, Jennie		1866	1939
, Bailey		12- 7-1890	9-16-1914

---

*Robert Foster Johnson, M.A., is a native of Casey County and is a retired public school teacher.

HAMILTON, W. H.		1-23-1881	9-22-1927
HAWKINS, Tommie	husband	1893	
, Drusilla B.	wife	1875	1947
HEIGHTCHEW, Davie		6-15-1910	5- 5-1931
HUGHES, America T.	w. of W. P.	1827	1881
, W. P.		2-23-1819	4-19-1895
, James M.		6-17-1856	9- 9-1894
, Wm. T.		1914	1914
, Mattie S.		1892	1923
JAMES, Mary Jane		1877	1950
KEITH, Charles Ora		10- 3-1860	4- 6-1950
KELLEY, Samuel R.		1868	1944
, Sarah A.	w. of S. R	1873	1956
KEPHART, Aunt June			
, L. J. Aynes		1861	1944
MILES, L. W.		8-15-1861	3- 5-1924
, Nancy		3-11-1868	1- 9-1965
O'NAN, Enoch		1897	1955
PAYTON, John B.		1879	1937
, Lena M.	w. of J. B.	1883	
SHAW, John		1846	1918
, Mary F.		1849	1935
STIVERS, Lucy A.		10- 1-1861	7-30-1928
, Henry S.		7- 6-1858	6-15-1922
THURMOND, John		8-22-1852	
, Ed		1-22-1894	
, Agnes O'Brien	w. of Ed	4- 6-1894	1-19-1938
, Mary Catherine	w. of John	4-30-1857	1- 8-1921
TROXELL, Thomas		1853	1917
, Sarah H.		1850	1914
TURNER, Reuben	s. of R. W. & S. A.	1-10-1879	8-31-1891
WADE, Thomas		6- 8-1857	6- 8-1907

57. Franklinton Baptist Church Cemetery.
Franklinton, Kentucky.

ADAMS, Mary S.	w. of G. H.	4-27-1836	6-13-1881
, Nancy M.		1859	1904
, Thos. L.		1883	1907
ALDRIDGE, Ethel Colston		1901	1966
, Lindon		1882	1953
, Ollie B.	w. of Lindon	1881	1936
BAKER, Rachael	d. of Samuel Jones	10-29-1830	11-5 -1886
BARTON, T. H.		1862	1936
, Annie E.		1866	1949
, Nathan		1830	1903
, Mary E.		9- 2-1836	9- 2-1887
, Ira P.		1892	1954
, Nora J.	w. of I. P.	1895	
BEETEM, Nancy E.	w. of J. M.	10- 2-1838	8- 7-1881
, James M.		7-14-1835	10-23-1906
BLACKABY, Step		1880	1950
, Myrtle	w. of Step	1886	19--
, Guthrie		1907	1953
, Anna Leah	w. of Guthrie	1910	
, Mattie Bell		1878	1961
, J. W.		1877	1949
, Sarah Edna		1877	1927
BRIERLY, Robert T.		1881	1971
, Manda T.	w. of R. T.	1885	
BRYANT, Dave		1866	1930
, Lucy	w. of Dave	1874	1954
, L. S.		1846	1928
, Nobel N.		1874	
, Mary M.	w. of N. N.	1879	1950
BULLOCK, Levi J.	killed	6- 7-1853	7- 5-1873
BUSH, Albert Reese	bur. on the old family farm	1842	1872
, Nancy Jane Clubb	w. of A. R.	1843	1924
, Ella Bryant		12- 5-1872	1-27-1956

Name	Relation	Born	Died
, James William		5- 2-1867	6-12-1948
, Thomas B.		1869	1953
, Sallie A.		1871	1953
, Anderson		1878	1943
CASEY, Joseph T.		1862	1949
, Sarah	w. of J. T.	1866	1921
, Eliza Jane		1882	1950
, James M.		1888	1969
, Nettie Scriber	w. of J. M.	1889	1965
CLUBB, Mary	w. of F.		
, Harvey S.		1839	1918
, Martha F.	w. of H. S.	1839	1924
, Orkley		1883	1943
COLLETT, Isaac		1829	1909
, Mary Ann	w. of Isaac	1828	1907
COLSTON, Arch		3- 4-1859	5-28-1916
, Lidda	w. of A.	6-18-1874	
CRAVENS, Earl		1900	1966
, Clyde M.		1904	
, James A.		1858	1926
, Allie J.		1867	1938
DILLMAN, Polly Ann	w. of Vachel	1816	1850
DOUGLAS, John		1892	1953
, Ethel J.	w. of John	1893	19--
DOUGLASS, Elizabeth		1898	1901
, Elizeann		1869	1901
DOWDEN, George		1805	1900
, Martha M.	w. of George	1807	1882
, Wm.		3-19-1835	2-26-1908
, Zachary Taylor		1847	1928
, Belle Massie		1851	1929
DUNAWAY, Lego		1884	1918
, Lillie	w. of Lego	1886	1967
, Charlie		1887	1968
, Maud	w. of Charley	1891	1931
ELLEGOOD, J.		9-22-1820	2-27-1892
, Martha		10-15-1825	3-28-1890
ELSTON, Joseph		7- 9-1809	1-12-1894
ERWIN, Corlie A.		1884	1945
, Virginia L.	w. of Corlie A.	1888	
EWING, John		1839	1928
, Catherine	w. of John	1843	1920
, Herbert		1873	1936
, Bettie	w. of Herbert	1874	
GARDNER, John E.		3-17-1868	9- 2-1913
, Florence	w. of J. E.	11- 3-1868	6- 7-1930
, J. Ola		1888	1954
, Emma H.	w. of J. O.	1889	1958
, Willie		1891	1958
, Rosa E.	w. of Willie	1893	1970
, James H.		4- 4-1865	8- 7-1953
, Luvenia T. Malin	w. of J. H.	3- 8-1863	7- 4-1928
, Prentice C.		1892	1928
GREEN, William		1848	1939
, Drusilla		1851	1938
, Arvenia Jones		1858	1933
, Robert		1850	1901
, Joseph		1881	1911
, Cora E.		1879	1943
HALL, H. T.	w. of S.	10-21-1847	3-23-1877
HANCE, Sarah K.	w. of W. J.	11-25-1849	8-20-1882
HARTFORD, W. R.		5- 3-1808	6- 7-1892
, Betsy T.	w. of W. R.	1813	8- 9-1888
HEATON, Richard W.		12-15-1834	1-16-1894
, Wm. Douglas		1860	1942
, Margaret		1864	1936
, T. D.		1- 2-1852	12-21-1882
, Edna	w. of T. D.	8-27-1852	11-24-1912
HOLMES, David S.		1876	1947

Name	Remarks	Born	Died
, Edna J.		1889	1965
, Leonard G.	WW II	1920	1944
HUKILL, W. E., Jr.		9-12-1883	11-15-1930
, Jennie		1885	1951
JONES, Samuel		10-29-1830	11- 5-1886
, Lucinda	w. of Samuel	7- 1-1803	9-12-1873
, Daniel, Sr.		3- 8-1775	9-16-1850
, Clarence		1882	1928
, James P.		1855	
, Addie	w. of James P.	1858	1927
, Louis H.		1864	1932
, Hallie	w. of L. H.	1863	
, Albert		5- 2-1849	4- 2-1930
, Wm.		10-14-1832	8-28-1904
, Ray		1906	
, Elizabeth	w. of Ray	1908	1940
, Abram		1817	1896
, Catherine		1819	1896
, D. P.		1865	1934
, Lydia	w. of D. P.	1865	1934
, S. F.		1841	1925
, Lucinda J.	w. of S. F.	1847	1937
, Alfred		1894	1967
, Grace	w. of Alfred	1900	
, Harvey		1868	1943
, Stasie	w. of Harvey	1871	1964
, Frank		1872	1956
, Mattie		1879	1920
, Chester		1898	
, Myrtle		1896	
, Will		1877	1937
, Eliza	w. of Will	1868	1953
, John L.		1881	
KALUSY, Boyd D.		1902	1932
, Nick		1873	1931
, Julia	w. of Nick	1879	1954
LINDSAY, Amanda	w. of Tolbert	9- 3-1841	6-27-1870
, Nathaniel		2-14-1797	1- 2-1872
, Mary		10-14-1803	3-28-1896
, Sarah E.	w. of Edwin	8-21-1835	4- 8-1882
, Edwin		1832	1904
LOUDEN, Willie B.		1870	1937
, Sallie	w. of W. B.	1869	
McGOWAN, America Dowden	w. of M. J.	1-25-1833	11-29-1898
, W. F. & D. T.			
McGREW, D. T.		1859	1930
, Annie	w. of D. T.	1867	
MEEK, John Samuel		1855	1933
, Lydia Francis	w. of J. S.	1860	1904
MUIR, Burton		10- 6-1915	1-21-1966
NEWMAN, George A.		1865	
, Cordelia	w. of G. A.	1872	1933
NOLIN, Lego L.		1885	1965
, Bessie B.	w. of L. L.	1887	1965
, Ray W.		1909	1943
, Dorothy	w. of R. W.	1920	19--
PARDO, S. A.		1854	1937
, Mary O.	w. of S. A.	3-25-1861	4- 6-1903
, Price		1886	1936
, Fannie	w. of Price	1894	
PYNE, Wm. H.		1900	1968
RAINS, H. S.		1865	1953
, Kate	w. of H. S.	1871	1928
RAISOR, Frank M.		1855	1917
, Anna B.	w. of F. M.	1866	1908
, Jesse L.		1875	1949
, Mary E. Toner	w. of J. L.	1874	1957
ROBERTS, John		10- 4-1831	4-24-1890
, J. M.		1844	
, Sarah M.	his wife	10- 1-1845	

Mrs. Paul Dent

Old Richard Callaway family cemetery, Henry County.

Name		Born	Died
, Willie		1889	1921
, Myrtle	w of Willie	1891	1955
, Donald C.		1938	1954
, Jessie Lee		1870	1942
, Margaret B.	w. of J. L.		
, Sylvanus		1868	1958
, Alice H.	w. of Sylvanus		
RODGERS, George J.		1877	1953
, Margaret A.		1879	1963
ROSE, Valerie		1870	1943
, Arch		1865	1928
, Emma		1891	1939
SCRIBER, Orem		1894	1924
, Mary K.		1896	1960
, Bernard		1887	1950
, John		4-24-1859	8-11-1896
SHELLEY, Daniel		11- -1815	1-30-1880
, John, Sr.		1848	1926
SMITH, Mary	w. of L. T.	12-23-1839	1- 4-1929
, Louis T.		5- 2-1832	10-19-1919
, Lora Huey		1883	1955
, John M.		1884	1947
, Martha E.	w. of John M.	1888	1970
SORENSON, Mabel C.		1900	
STIVERS, Jesse		1905	
, M. Leona	w. of Jesse	1906	1970

Name	Note	Born	Died
THOMAS, Lee V.		1874	1941
, Mattie C.	w. of L. V.	1881	1931
THOMPSON, Nancy		1825	1876
TINGLE, Lego		9- 1-1880	3- 9-1968
, Sylvester O.		1881	1957
, Drucilla	w. of S. O.	1891	1929
, Mary J.		1887	1910
, Wm. Herman		8-18-1895	11- 5-1959
, Lydia White	w. of B. W.	6-16-1877	1-24-1957
, Hessie Collett		1873	1902
, Barton W.		1866	1941
, Leonard A.		1885	1964
, Clara W.	w. of L. A.	1896	1943
, Leonard		1870	1938
, Lizzie H.	w. of Leonard	1876	1960
, Alvis		1873	1945
, Lizzie	w. of Alvis	1886	1970
WAINSCOTT, George E.		1879	1958
, Mary W.	w. of G. E.	1885	1948
WELSH, Callie		1879	1968
, Preston		1881	1952
, Joseph		1839	1904
WELTY, Lutie T.	his wife	10-16-1878	1-18-1911
, D. A.		4- 6-1873	
WHITEFIELD, Sarah J.	w. of J. V.	1864	1941
, James V.		1860	1953
WOOLDREDGE, Caroline		1842	1922
WYATT, Nina		1913	1915

58. Campbellsburg Public Cemetery.

Name	Note	Born	Died
ABBOTT, Lev. G.		1864	1952
, Naomi P.	his wife	1870	1958
ANDERSON, James P.		1861	1947
, Millie B.		1866	1933
ANTILL, Peter D.	a. 51 y.		1890
ARNOLD, J. Perry		1845	1878
, Anna P.		1851	1937
, James		4- 9-1811	2- 5-1891
, C. W.		1809	1893
, Lucy		1815	1907
, W. J.	Co. F, 8 Ky. Cav., CSA		
ASHER, Alonza	s. of M. & M.	1857	1879
BACKUS, Wm.		1813	1880
BALL, Geo. Affy		1875	1958
, Anna Pearl		1889	1929
, Charlie A.		1883	1956
, Nannie C.	his wife	1888	1959
BARNETT, James C.		1823	1906
, Margaret O.	his wife	1841	1916
, Harold T.		1909	1964
, Lenora F.	w. of H. T.	1911	
, Ashby		1879	1949
, Cora	his wife	1882	1970
, Angie C.		1876	1896
, J. T.		1835	1920
, Martha	his wife	1846	1928
, C. E.		1869	1930
, W. L.		1867	1913
, Mary Jo.		1934	1947
, Raymond R.		1906	1969
, Mary Dean		1906	
, Major L.		1875	1958
, Grace R.	his wife	1881	1964
, Arthur		1879	1967
, John Elias		1866	1958
, Benona	his wife	1881	1961
, Wm.		8-22-1861	10-28-1939
, Betty Berry	w. of Wm.	4-12-1858	1-18-1941

BATTS, Courtland		1905	1972
, Gladys	his wife	1907	
, Thomas B.		1885	1950
, Cleo G.	his wife	1889	1964
, Harold		1912	1919
BAXTER, Ellen	w. of Pascal	1855	1904
BECKLEY, Clarence H.		1889	1960
, Mary Alice	w. of C. H.	1892	1919
, James R.		1867	1934
, Mary T.	his wife	1867	1949
, Joe		1893	
, Delia	his wife	1890	1947
BELL, Nannie Cutting		1875	1943
, Cornelia Wigginton	w. of Ambrose	1831	1906
, Ambrose		4- 2-1825	
BERRY, Wm. Grant		1833	1909
, Jennie Stubbins	w. of W. G.	1833	1881
, Elizabeth Bush	w. of Allen	1811	1871
, Estil D.		1874	1959
, Gertrude M.	his wife	1884	1953
BEVARLY, Vernon		1881	1958
, Russie	his wife	1882	1964
, Raymond W.		9-11-1905	11- 1-1937
, Samuel W.		11-19-1873	7-18-1945
, Angeline, A.		1875	1921
BISHOP, Will		1866	1917
, Ollie	his wife	1876	1931
BLACKABY, Wm. S.		1904	
, Bertha M.	his wife	1906	1952
BOULWARE, S. O.		1-26-1849	5-13-1919
, Lethe A.	w. of S. O.	8-29-1856	10-24-1910
BOYER, Sterling Price		6-12-1856	3-16-1932
, James		9- 1-1824	2- 8-1905
, Eliza Ellen	w. of J.	8-10-1838	3-11-1875
, Leslie N.		1856	1922
, Rena	his wife	1864	1948
, Dr. Wm. F.		1921	1962
, Wm. A.		1863	1945
, Bettie	his wife	1862	1921
BRADSHAW, Sarah Orem		1910	1943
BRENT, James Thomas		1866	1938
, Minnie Francis	his wife	1869	1949
, Valora J.		1867	1908
, E. W.		1883	1968
, Oveta	his wife	1884	1957
, Dewey Floyd		1900	1964
, Anna B.		1904	1958
, Nannie H.	w. of D. T. a. 27 y.		1835
, Dale Allen		1872	1954
, Ella B.		1871	1952
, Ira A.		1875	1936
, Minnie L.		1879	1965
, Joseph N.		1862	1926
, Mary T.		1841	1928
, Lizzie A.		1870	1928
, Joseph W.		1911	1946
, Raymond		1900	1943
, James		1866	
, Thomas		1838	
, Minnie		1869	
, Francis			
, Arthur H.		1904	1956
, W. T.		1881	1963
, Cora	his wife	1880	1956
, Newton D.		1867	1936
, Noble A.		1890	1953
, Nettie B.	his wife	1890	
, Leland		1880	1950
, Anna M.		1880	1965

Name	Note	Born	Died
, Willie		1884	1962
, Roxie	his wife	1888	1956
BREWER, R. Pratt		1885	1960
, Ruth	his wife	1893	
BRIGHT, Wm. Henry		1860	1928
, Fannie J.		1873	1959
BROWN, Eva		1892	1958
, Francis		1858	1943
, Blue		1859	1922
, Thomas J.		1885	1902
, Mabel L.		1880	1895
, Fannie M.		1846	1895
, Mattie P.		1-10-1882	
, Dee M.		1892	1970
, Rosa	his wife	1898	
BRYANT, Wm. S.		1885	1950
, T. C.		1836	1920
, Zerhelda	w. of T. C.	1846	1918
, Elisha F.		1812	1883
, Frances		1814	1886
, Mary Berry	w. of A. W.	1864	1901
, A. W.		1855	1938
, Avo		1895	1896
, Lewis Harrison		1851	1907
, Anna Kinnear	w. of L. H.	1851	1925
, Sallie May		1890	1918
, Ova		1895	1921
, Ella		1863	1944
, Nancy O.	w. of M. E.	1817	1875
, M. E.		1811	1892
, Henry		1887	1953
, Eugene		1921	
, Ethel		1890	19--
, Faye		1919	1972
, James N.		1884	1967
, Sadie C.	w. of J. N.	1881	1955
, Elisha F.		2-26-1812	3-27-1883
, Frances		8-20-1814	5- 7-1886
, H. E.		10-30-1811	10-19-1892
BURGE, Eva R.	w. of G. E.	1889	
, George E.		1879	1955
BUSH, Martha V.		1915	1968
, Joseph A.		1914	1972
CAIN, Charles M.		1873	1950
, Maud B.	his wife	1888	1967
CALLIS, George		1892	1961
, Nettie B.		1898	1955
CALVIN, Jesse		1875	1955
CAMPBELL, Levi		1821	1877
, Joseph Morris		1865	1953
, Katie Voiers		1868	1946
, Mary J.	w. of J. H.	1837	1929
, Joseph H.		1827	1906
, Wallace Voiers		1892	1964
, Wm.			1959
, Laura	his wife		1959
, John E.		1832	1908
, Ruth A.	his wife	1833	1907
, E. P.		1829	1870
, James	a. 96 y.		3-14-1889
, Zerilda	w. of James	1820	1868
, Nannie			
, J. F.		1875	1912
, James Denton		1902	1955
, Samuel A.		1868	1944
, James L.		1862	
, Nannie T.		1862	1937
, Wm. S.		1830	1901
, George T.		1815	1878
, Ann E.		1818	1900

Name		Born	Died
, Martha	w. of Wm.	1833	1872
, Joseph H.		7-21-1857	3-10-1879
, Thos. E.		8- 7-1863	11-29-1906
, Lora V.	his wife	8-17-1873	8-31-1915
, Milton			1934
, Parthenia		1837	1931
, Joseph H.		1827	1906
, Mary J.	his wife	1837	1929
, Joseph Morris		1865	1953
, Levi		12- 9-1821	11-17-1877
, E. P.		12-25-1829	8- 6-1870
, Martha	w. of Wm.	10- 7-1823	12-22-1872
CAPLINGER, Minnie Arnold	w. of J. L.	1873	1938
CARDER, Bartlett		1871	1946
, Minnie A.	his wife	1876	1944
, Tice		1887	1972
, Bessie	his wife	1888	1937
, Gilbert		1914	1963
, Donald R.		1939	1969
, Love		1876	1959
, Lora W.		1893	
CARR, Almira		1868	1905
CHAPMAN, Wilbert L.		1900	
, Lillian	his wife	1903	
CHILTON, Lawrence		1854	1935
, Ellen	w. of L.	1859	1939
, Alvin A.		1884	1966
, Nettie D.		1886	1972
, Wm. T.		1877	1957
, Achie M.	his wife	1885	1965
, Bettie		1878	1962
, Harry		1890	
, Ethel	his wife	1892	1959
, Louis		1878	1966
, Mary A.	his wife	1880	1950
CLARK, Wm.		1883	1966
, Anna Dora		1887	1946
COBLIN, Louis		1852	1940
, St. Elmo		1884	1929
, Pearl Dawkins	w. of St. E.	1883	1952
, Dr. W. T.		1848	1907
, Ella		1872	1924
CONTI, Mary Augusta N.		12-11-1879	
COOMBS, Wm. Pryor		1833	1905
CORBIN, Vernon		1889	1958
, Guthrie		1887	1947
, Silas		1851	1910
, Louisa C.		1846	1906
, Willie C.		1870	1896
, L. Scott		1894	1953
, Andrew J.		1874	1918
, Georgia F.		1876	1960
, Mayme Stivers	w. of Lemuel	1891	1947
, Lemuel		1889	1969
, James William		1854	1933
, Hallie Goode		1860	1952
, Charlie Goode		1902	1964
, Charles S.		7- 7-1857	5- 4-1897
CULLEN, James		1860	1917
, Harriett E.	w. of J.	1860	1940
CUNNINGHAM, Edward B.		1854	1921
DARRAH, Jesse M.		3-26-1841	
DAVIS, Wm.		1907	1971
, Rebecca	his wife	1904	
DAWKINS, George W.		1849	1926
, Bettie S.	w. of George W.	1853	1937
DEMAREE, James Wesley		1872	1913
, Allie		1884	
, Dora M.		1880	1940
, Samuel		1834	1917

DEMPSEY, Frank		1880	1950
, Howard C.	WW II	1913	1944
, Joseph S.		1814	1878
, Chas. S.		1855	1883
DENN, Thos. B.		1882	1944
, Sue M.	his wife	1881	1944
DOWNS, Ben X.		1877	1929
, Grace Scott			5- 4-1923
DUGAN, Joe B.		1902	
, Mary M.	his wife	1898	1951
DUNAWAY, John T.		1913	1968
, Kathryn	his wife	1918	
, Mary M.		1886	1928
DUNCAN, Herbert B.		1895	1971
, Marie B.	his wife	1900	
, Thomas J.		1870	1948
, Alice W.		1874	1963
EAST, Cora		1867	1895
, Susan		1818	1892
EDMONDSON, Lucie		1889	1912
, Mary Lee		1854	1895
EDRINGTON, Weldon B.		1871	1959
, Cordia	his wife	1871	1955
, Roy F.		1904	
, Virginia K.		1909	1969
ETHINGTON, Pearl Scott			11-23-1958
, Auburn R.			1956
FERGUSON, Walter A.		1876	1957
, Lucinda	his wife	1886	
, J. W.		1849	

Mrs. Paul Dent

Smithfield Cemetery, Henry County.

FEWELL, Marvin L.		1910	
, Ruth W.		1918	
, James Jake		1902	1960
, Lillian		1909	1970
, Annie	w. of Kirby	1876	1915
, Kirby		1874	1939
FOREE, James W.		1835	1885
, Malvina		1839	1926
, Thomas S.		1817	1877
, M. Amanda		1824	1893
GARDNER, Louisa	w. of John	1829	1859
GARRIOTT, John F.		10-13-1837	3-25-1906
, Wilbur		1882	1943
, Daniel		1845	1915
, Nancy Ellen	his wife	1851	1924
, Emma B.		1873	1961
, W. R.		1869	1917
, Belle		1864	1939
, Simeon		1840	1883
, Grant K.		1951	
GIDDENS, Jesse W.		1868	1927
GIVENS, Lora M.		1874	1915
GIVIDEN, Bettie		1859	1914
, Robert W.		1867	1934
, Belle S.		1896	
, Mary E.		1836	1918
, Jennie		1885	1914
, Emma K. Mitchell	w. of J. H.	1861	1943
, John A.		1864	1951
, Flora	w. of J. A.	1871	1951
GOLEY, Thos. J.		4- 8-1917	
GOODE, Lemuel		9-13-1833	3-18-1901
, Nannie	his wife	2- 5-1835	12-30-1900
GOODRUM, J. G.		1840	1924
, Rachael	his wife	1839	1912
GOODWIN, Vernon		1893	1953
, Lillian	his wife	1905	1944
GUTTING, Eliza F.	w. of N.	1843	1880
HAMILTON, J. Sidney		1873	1944
, Dullie L.	his wife	1875	1960
HANCOCK, Martha Ann		1843	1922
, Robert Asa		1840	1914
, A. B.		1850	1882
HARDESTY, Richard		1845	1922
, Mary	his wife	1846	1921
, Scottie		1884	1913
, Sarah E.	w. of Moses	1838	1876
, Oscar M.		1907	1972
, Dorothy		1909	
HARGROVE, Wm.		1896	1959
, Lillian	his wife	1900	
HAVETER, Margaret E.		1872	1952
HAYDEN, Geo. A.		1850	1930
, Dee F.		1851	1920
, Levi		1889	1958
HEILMAN, Roy C.		1925	1967
, Wm. C.		1924	1965
, Peggy H.		1931	
, Raymond L.		1903	1959
, Margaret B.		1904	
HILL, Wm. N.		1854	1934
, Mary E.	w. of W. N.	1864	1922
, Juanita L.		1890	1965
HILTON, A. J.		1848	1919
HISLE, James	b. Va.	1-10-1803	8-22-1880
, Mary D.		1834	1914
HOPKINS, Noble		1901	1964
, Mattie	his wife	1904	
HOSLEY, Lewis		1881	1948
, Elva	his wife	1882	1937

Name	Note	Born	Died
HUFFMAN, Pauline Bishop		1906	1967
HUMPSTON, Noble G.		1879	1918
Leonora Sams		1859	1927
, Dr. O. M.		1851	1914
JACKSON, Joel		5- 4-1851	4- 9-1932
, Josie Hagan	w. of Joel	1864	1938
, Susan E.		7-15-	12- 5-
, Mary M.		1819	1901
, Rowland		5- 5-1814	1-31-1888
, John O.		1853	1911
, James		1847	1921
JEFFRIES, Nannie Campbell		1877	1895
, Willard		1859	1893
, James		1824	1879
, Calvin		1853	1929
, Mary	his wife	1858	1913
, J. T.		1882	1949
JENKINS, Clarence L.		1873	1952
, Cassandra	his wife	1880	1966
JEWELL, G. T.		1850	1880
JONES, Thos. P.		1828	1897
, Letitia	his wife	1832	1921
, Joseph T.		1860	1929
, Affie Alice		1861	1931
, Irvin Thomas		1887	1929
, Burton		1896	1962
, Dalton W.		1891	1968
, Mary W.	his wife	1891	1968
JUSTICE, Omer D.		1879	1960
, Beulah L.		1896	
, James L.		1935	1973
, Juanita	his wife	1940	1973
KELLY, Sarah Frances		1843	1908
, Samuel		1842	1895
KINDOLL, Iris Kathryn		1920	1880
LaMASTER, Ben		1827	1900
, John T.		1858	1927
, Ben I.		1868	1956
, Emily		7- 1-1829	10-21-1894
, Letitia	w. of Abraham	6-19-1800	4-18-1885
, Joanna	d. of A. &. L.	11-21-1837	6-30-1859
LAW, Frank A.		1871	1950
, Mary E.		1872	1950
LEE, James W.		1818	1881
, James W.		1914	
, Ella Ransdell		1933	
, Wm. H.		1846	1927
, Sophia		1844	1901
, Levi Marion		1847	1920
, Elizabeth Caplinger		1861	1942
LIST, Martha	w. of J. L.	1841	1967
LITER, Affie M.	w. of W. T. d. of W. F. & C. J. Ransdell	1882	1908
, Dora		1876	1956
, Carrie B.	w. of W. T. d. of W. F. & C. J. Ransdell	1887	1911
, Anita	w. of W. T. d. of F. M. & H. Foree	1881	1934
, W. T.		1876	19--
, Minnie Turner	w. of W. T.	1882	1953
, Perry F.		1871	1939
LOCKART, Hattie R.		1881	1916
LOUDEN, J. Howard		1907	
, Sarah V.	his wife	1909	1969
LUCKETT, Elias M.		1843	1910
, Lucy	his wife	1848	1919
LUDLOW, John		1909	1972
, Gladys M.	his wife	1911	
McCLELLAN, W. O., Sr.		1886	1956
, Alpha M.	his wife	1898	1949

Name	Note	Born	Died
McINTIRE, Cortez		1878	
, Minnie A.	his wife	1870	1954
McQUILLEN, Cornelia Jewell			
MAHONEY, John L.		1899	1968
, Addie M.	w. of J. L.	1909	
, Scottie B.		1878	1951
, Ashby		1872	1950
, Annie E.	his wife	1874	1941
, Cline A.		1904	1962
, Eva J.	w. of C. A.	1909	
, Wm. B.		1878	1963
, Nellie J.	his wife	1881	1945
MARQUIS, Nellie C.		2- 1-1892	10- 3-1909
MARTINI, John		1-20-1833	1- 2-1913
, Letha Nash	w. of John	12-10-1837	12-20-1891
, Oscar		1884	1916
MARTINIE, Wm. P.		11-20-1866	5-24-1958
, Ella S.	w. of W. P.	1-31-1880	
MATHIS, Howard J.		1905	1954
, Margaret E.		1909	
, Howard J.	killed in Korea	1929	1951
MAY, Charles O.		1902	1967
, Hallie L.	w. of C. O.	1905	
, Wm. M.		1881	1944
, Julia E.	his wife	1885	
MEADOWS, Noah T.		1882	1968
, Ora Bell	his wife	1906	1969
MINOR, W. E.		1868	1915
MITCHELL, T. A.		1-15-1835	2-19-1918
, Elvree	w. of T. A.	11- 4-1842	4-18-1926
, R. L.		1879	1965
, Sallie P.	his wife	1881	1964
, Jacob Arthur		1872	1963
, Lula W.		1879	1965
MONFORT, Wm.		1816	1858
, Bettie	w. of Geo. D.	1844	1878
, Flora	w. of Geo. D.	1855	1886
, Geo. D.		1846	1927
, Carrie R.		1858	1953
, Ben L.		1877	
, Lydia C.		1872	1956
, Frank H.		1902	
, Irene E.		1911	1968
, Wm.		10-24-1816	7-15-1856
, Flora	w. of Geo.	7-25-1855	8-28-1885
MONROE, James A.		1878	1958
MOORE, Wm. P.		1862	1938
, Maggie P.		1867	1943
, Walter C.		1864	1928
, Mary E.		1899	1916
, J. S.		1885	1937
, Ora W	his wife	1889	1958
NEAL, Edward M.		1873	1937
, Annie	w. of W. M.	1874	1928
NEIL, Dorothy C.		1900	1971
NEILL, J. Stanley		1890	
NELSON, Curtis		1910	1951
, Callie	his wife	1914	
, Chester		1917	1970
, Mamie	his wife	1920	
NETHERLAND, Vera		1889	1899
, Richard C.		1854	1925
, Bettie Parker		1864	1951
, Wm. G.		1887	1951
, Martha B.		1918	1918
, Lutie		1-22-1881	
, Georgia		1858	1884
NEWBY, Herbert		3-28-1916	
, David McFarland		1853	1930
, Sarah Jane	his wife	1855	1952

NORVELL, Charles S.		1882	1938
, Maude W.	his wife	1879	1963
, Sinnett D.		1870	1936
, Dora	his wife	1886	
OGDEN, Vernon Calvin		1944	
OREM, Fowler		1860	1892
, Nannie D.	his wife	1863	1895
, Ira Bryant		1875	1949
, Addie Dawkins	w. of I. B.	1876	1937
, Joseph		1832	1900
, Lucy Ann	w. of Joseph	1838	1872
, Sallie F.	2nd w. of Joseph	1843	1912
, Mal Lee		1878	1962
, Alice Green	w. of Mal	1877	1969
, Charles		1877	1963
, Helen A.	his wife	1893	
ORR, J. P.		1834	1916
, Margaret	his wife	1843	1918
OWEN, Wm. H.		1882	1960
, Ethel B.	his wife	1883	1968
PEAK, Sally E.	w. of I. N.	1846	1882
, Isaac N.		1844	1937
, Mattie G.	his wife	1857	1952
, Frances	w. of Wm.	5-20-1814	12-27-1885
PENDLETON, Irvin		6-28-1896	1- 4-1962
, George H.		1873	1947
, Mary N.		1879	1965
, Lonnie B.		1869	1950
PENISTON, Wm. H.		1833	1919
, Maria C.	w. of Wm. H.	1847	1939
PERKINS, Bunnie D.		1884	1943
POE, Wm. T.		1891	1959
, Lawrence		1891	
, Rose	his wife	1889	
POPP, James		1872	1953
, Allie		1876	1943
, Herbert, Jr.		1941	
, Linda G.	his wife	1948	1971
POWELL, Robert N.		1848	1918
, Leonora	his wife	1859	1931
, James	66th y.		3- 3-1877
PYLE, Robert Lynn		1941	
, Nellie Lee			7-26-1959
PYLES, W. H.		1835	1917
, Lucia	w. of W. H.	1844	1917
, Clarence		1880	1958
, Ella	his wife	1879	1955
, Oscar H., Jr.	USN		
, Maud Jeffries		1880	1944
, O. A.		1876	1930
, Mary C.		1847	1925
RADCLIFF, John Carroll		1894	1956
, Mary Elizabeth	bur. 2-15-1974	1892	
RAINS, Raymond M.		1902	
, Cleo R.	his wife	1904	1950
, Edgar E.		1863	1928
, Carrie	w. of E. E.	1872	1912
RAISOR, Russell L.		1899	1963
, Mabel Claire		1902	
, Thomas F.		1867	1948
, Maud L.	his wife	1873	1957
RANSDELL, Wm. F.		1854	1936
, Eliza		1807	1884
, John C.		1863	1931
, Clarence S.		1867	1961
, Ida Mae		1871	1945
, Betty		1859	1958
, John C.		1825	1881
, Cora J.	w. of W. F. d. of J. S. & A. J. Fallis	1861	1911

REPTKA, Barnta		1832	1909
, Lucy E.	his wife	1841	1915
RICHMOND, James E.		1913	1967
, Effie C.	his wife	1888	1963
, Bertha		1893	
, Elliott A.	WW II	1914	1944
, Felt		1883	1942
, Isabel	his wife	1893	
, James A.		1874	
, Minnie L.	his wife	1876	1939
ROBBINS, Aggie		1890	1948
, Dora		1883	1962
, Georgia Ann		1912	1944
ROBERSON, John T.		1843	1899
, Sallie		1846	1923
, R. A.		1837	1912
, Beany	w. of R. A.	1845	1913
, Lee		1873	1936
, Maggie		1879	1951
ROBERTS, Cassius C.		1851	1925
, Tuscumba		1859	1921
, Leslie		1881	1965
, Betty		1885	
, Harrison		1828	1870
ROBINSON, Ruby Brent		1910	1973
ROBISON, Pearl Sue		1905	1938
, Mary Elizabeth		1877	1962
ROGERS, Naomi P.		12-10-1850	1-13-1916
SAMS, Griffin		5- 2-1831	5- 2-1917
, Elizabeth	w. of G.	1834	1912
SANDERS, James C.		1878	1966
, Anna W.	his wife	1878	1947
, B. C.		1882	1970
SANDIFER, Lizzie C.		1868	1920
, Elizabeth	a. 67 y.		1892
SCOTT, Milton Levy		1844	1925
, Chilton		1813	1894
, Mary Campbell	w. of C.	1825	1904
, George M.		1895	1955
, Hallie B.	w. of G. M.	1897	
, Roland T.			
, John T.			
, Anna E.			
, Maggie Z.			
, Frank L.		1894	1967
, Elizabeth P.		1871	1955
, James Robert		1863	1940
, Mattie Osborn		1877	1934
, Emma A.		1845	1910
, Wm. C.		1865	1894
, Mary E.		1886	1970
, L. B.		1858	1929
, Mattie	w. of L. B.		
, Chas. T.		1824	1901
, Lizzie Goslee	w. of C. T.	1827	1884
, Elizabeth A.		1883	1950
, James G.		1853	1927
, Cora M.		1853	1948
, Minnie S.		1852	1928
, E. C.		1851	1914
, James B.		9- 3-1810	1-14-1871
, Rachael	w. of J. B.	1807	1867
, Mary Jane	w. of W. F.	12-22-1839	4-29-1885
, Kate Morris		1849	1932
SEARCY, Inez		1875	1960
, Harry		1875	1947
SHEPHERD, Mancy Ree		1873	1934
, Clara M.	w. of W. F.	1853	1942
, John Edward		1889	1948

Mrs. Paul Dent

Smithfield Cemetery, Henry County.

Name	Note	Born	Died
, Bessie Stivers	w. of J. E.	1889	
	d. of J. T. & S. M.		
SHOUP, Mary H.	wife	1843	1921
, Samuel B.	husband	1840	1903
SIDEBOTTOM, Kenneth		1919	1952
SIMPSON, Fillmore		1876	1962
SINGLETON, Laura M.		1895	1963
, Charles S.		1871	1944
, Lena T.		1877	1917
, Frances	w. of Boyce	1895	1921
SKIDMORE, Will		1881	1963
, Minnie	w. of Will	1885	
SMITH, Bessie Ann	w. of James K.	1822	1864
, Mary J.	w. of J. K.	1830	1870
, M. W., Sr.		1854	1926
, Nannie		1859	1944
, Claude J.		1893	1953

SMITHERS, Wm. C.		1878	1942
STANLEY, Charley		1875	1946
, Nettie		1891	1968
STAPLES, Miles		1877	19--
, Pandora		1891	1941
STAPP, John S.		1830	1904
, Mattie Broadhurst	his wife	1840	1909
, Robert A.		1861	1888
STATEN, E. B.		1876	
, Fannie	his wife	1875	1961
, Maud		5-11-1886	
, Dora		1883	1938
, Inez		1890	
STRATTEN, Our Little		2-28-1856	1-22-1863
STROTHER, James R.		1868	1939
, Lydia D.	w. of J. R.	1874	1940
SULLIVAN, Orin Todd		1872	1932
, Hallie M.	w. of O. T.	1872	1961
, James W.		1915	1956
SUTER, Dr. Webb		1879	1939
, Edith	w. of Dr. W.	1883	
, John Wesley		1-28-1853	3-17-1937
, Mary Elizabeth	w. of J. W.	2-14-1857	11- 5-1942
, Wm. Wesley		1907	1943
SUTHERLAND, Billy E.		1931	1947
, Ashby		1903	1966
, Hallie	his wife	1900	
, Lue		1874	1937
, Warren		1868	1942
TANDY, Lewis E.		1886	1953
, Edd H.		1886	1971
, Edward H.		1919	1972
, Joan A.	his wife	1920	
TAYLOR, Chester		1890	1963
, Cordie	his wife	1893	
TEAGUE, Evan G.		1862	1912
, Carrie T.		1868	1907
THEOBALD, Rev. Lewis M.		1848	1914
, Fannie Crouch	his wife	1866	1958
THOMAS, Nathan G.		2-14-1831	6- 9-1901
, Sallie E.	his wife	5- 9-1836	2-11-1910
TILLER, Nolan T.		1906	1970
, Catherine	his wife	1917	
TINGLE, Marty C.		1886	
, Nora M.	his wife	1888	
TURNER, David			
, Carrie	his wife	1854	1908
, Wm. J.		1840	1936
, Frances K.	w. of W. J.	1850	1933
, Geo. M.		1873	1904
, J. Henry		1870	1901
TUTT, Martha J.	w. of J. R.	1821	1892
VORIES, Laura		1859	1934
, Wm. Tell		1857	1933
, Peter H.		1829	1908
, Sarah F.	w. of Peter	1835	1911
, Dr. W. L.		1863	1950
, Mary Turner	w. of Dr. W. L.	1866	1945
, Collie	w. of J. E.	1872	1917
WADE, Robert M.		1926	1971
, Sue O.	his wife	1934	
WALKER, Sanford		1858	1945
, Mattie	his wife	1852	1932
WEBB, Richard H.		1876	1955
, Maud S.	his wife	1880	
, Eugene		1904	
, Druscilla	his wife	1904	
, Isaac		1850	1925
, Jennie		1854	1937
, Dollie		1862	1925

Name	Notes	Born	Died
, Bettie		1870	1956
, Richard		1859	1937
, Wm.		1915	1945
WELLS, Sallie W.		1853	1929
WEST, Ed		1869	1941
, Georgia		1889	1951
WHITAKER, Will		2-28-1853	7- 2-1897
, Renda		1907	1956
, Ora		1853	1897
, Hanner E.	w. of Will	10- 6-1842	
WIGGINTON, Carrie E.		1884	1925
, J. Sidney		1884	1945
, Jesse E.		1881	1950
, Roy A.		1887	1953
, Berry W.		1838	1918
, Mary E.		1848	1917
, Wm. T.		1876	1909
, Fannie B.		1874	1909
WILLIAMS, Walden W.		1878	1910
, Geo. W.		1842	1911
, Mary E.	w. of G. W.	1847	1929
, Harland E.		1890	1939
, Carrie A.		1893	
, Tulla		1880	1956
, Zoda		1878	1969
WILSON, Georgia Lee		1880	1940
, Wm.		1874	1956
, Hallie C.	his wife	1876	1971
, Ada Brent		1877	1927
, Thos. A.		1878	1958
, Wm.		1876	1957
, Samuel K.		1838	1926
, Susan A.		1837	1919
WYATT, Taylor		1848	1934
, Fannie	his wife	1849	1909
, Mayme B.		1881	1908
YAGER, Franklin J.		1818	1912
, Diana Smith	w. of F. J.	1830	1899
, Dr. Walton H.		1868	1903
, Lucy L.		1851	1922

59. Chinn, Elley, Drane Cemetery
Russell Branch Road, near Point Pleasant

Name	Notes	Born	Died
BRANHAM, Martha T.	a. 28 y., 3 m., 22 d.		12-17-1828
, Edward	a. 34 y., 8 m., 26 d.		5-27-1829
BRINKER, Eliza Ann	a. 26 y., 1 m., 8 d.		11- 8-1830
, Morton	a. 26 y., 4 m.		8-25-1829
CHINN, Elijah	a. 32 y.		8- 1-1839
COWAN, Sarah Catherine	d. of John & Ann a. 5 y.		11-25-1821
, Mary Jane	d. of John & Ann a. 8 y., 9 m.		7-29-1818
DRANE, Infant son	s. of E. C. & J. C.		
DUPUY, Joseph	a. 50 y., 3 m., 14 d.		6-22-1815
, Mary N.	a. 17 y., 11 m., 1 d.		5- 5-1829
, John	a. 57 y.		
ELLEY, Henry		9-23-1808	10-23-1840
PRYOR, Mary	w. of W. S.	8-31-1824	8- 2-1854
SHIVELL, J. R.		3-25-1834	11-19-1863
SMITH, Mildred	d. of Z. F. & S.	1853	1854
, Zachariah		7- 9-1799	8-16-1826
, Joseph Dupuy	s. of Thos. & Harriett a. 1 y., 3 m., 22 d.		

60. Webb Cemetery.
Junction of Highways 1606 & 157, Sulphur.

MASON, Arthelia	s. of F. Bell	9-13-1890	3-10-1892
WEBB, Spencer		3- 4-1864	6-27-1891

61. McElwain Cemetery, Mr. Winters, owner.
S 1 m. off Hwy. 573, 4 m. E of New Castle.

McELWAIN, Nancy	w. of Wm.	3-17-1788	2-17-1874
, Wm.		3- 3-1786	9-17-1840
, W. T.		8-18-1826	10- 3-1837

62. Cureton Cemetery.
3 m. E of Point Pleasant Church.

BLACKWELL, Sarah C.		1810	1854
CURETON, James		10-17-1796	5-22-1873
, Nathaniel		1767	1850
, Elizabeth E.		1770	1837
, Henry		1808	1840

63. ½ m. W of Point Pleasant Church

KNIGHT, Jeremiah		10-14-1802	3-23-1872
, Amelia	w. of J.	9-12-1818	5- 1-1863

64. Bush Graveyard.
4 m. E of Point Pleasant.

BUSH, Albert Reese		11- 3-1842	8-10-1872
, Thomas			
, Pheba	d. of Albert R. & Nancy J.	6-16-1869	6-16-1869

65. Bartlett Graveyard.
½ m. S of Hwy. 66, 4 m. N of Point Pleasant Church.

BARTLETT, J. G.		1-21-1802	3-21-1881
, Hallie C.		1844	1865
PORTER, Carrie	d. of Larkin & Mattie	5- 4-1880	1-16-1881

66. Kephart Graveyard.
2 m. W of Bethlehem on Hwy. 22.

DITTO, Elzy		1866	1868
HALL, Eliza	w. of Wm. S.	9-15-1825	11- 8-1855
, William		7-17-1850	11- 8-1855
JOHNSTON, Lucy A.	d. of P. & F.	1836	1838
KELLY, Frances	w. of P. Johnston & J. Kelly	12- 1-1817	1- 2-1902
KEPHART, John W.		6-13-1854	2- 9-1894
, Thomas		6-20-1815	6- 3-1864
, Lydia		2- 4-1816	7-26-1859
, John		5-27-1824	4-27-1854
, Margaret	w. of John	12-10-1825	3-20-1862
, Abram		1-15-1787	5-21-1864
, Rebecca	w. of Abram	1784	1818
WELLS, Absalom S.		3-12-1793	1-20-1849

67. Kelly Graveyard, Mr. Moore, owner.
5 m. S of Lockport on Hensley Road.

CHISHOLM, John		4- 1-1874	12-12-1901
CLARK, Mariah	w. of Joe		
DOWNEY, Bernice		3-18-1893	12-25-1933

GILBERT, James W.		1847	1917
, M. J.		1858	
JAMES, Thomas		2-11-1848	4- 9-1921
, Aris		10-24-1823	11-11-1904
, Mary Jane	w. of Aris	8- 1-1824	
KELLY, Willie Daphne		1913	1919
, Daniel		6-20-1825	3- 1-1859
, Thomas		3-10-1856	3-12-1901
SHAW, Melissa A.	w. of S.	3-10-1854	1-25-1877
SMOOT, America	w. of Thomas	12-29-1826	11-19-1862

68. Church of Christ Graveyard.
1 m. S of Lockport on Carter's Road.

ALDRIDGE, Willard		1863	1934
, Sallie	his wife	1869	1934
MERIWETHER, L. A.		1889	1968
, Vinnie	his wife	1892	
NICHOLS, Cecil		1902	1948
REEVES, Saphronia	w. of J. W.	1854	1920
SUTHERLAND, Frank		1872	1938
, Melvina		1854	1934
WALLACE, Ellen		1- 6-1859	4-24-1886
, Thomas Cirley		5-15-1856	8-17-1909
WINTERS, Cassie E.		1893	1966
, Dan		9-30-1887	12-15-1938
, C. C.		1854	1928
, Cordelia		1856	1921

69. Erskine, Speed, Stivers, Sewell Cemetery, Eddie Beutel, owner.
Happy Ridge Road.

ERSKINE, Mary C.	w. of J. W. a. 62 y.		3-27-1898
FRAZIER, J. R.	....	1858	1891
HARP, Laurenia	w. of W. H.	1877	1900
JAMES, Bertha Pearl	w. of Geo.	1883	1904
SELF, Roxie L.	w. of Rinden	1882	1907
SEWELL, Thos. S.		1846	1899
, J. T.		1871	1922
, Hattie Pearl	w. of John	1881	1911
SPEED, James L.	s. of C. & J.	1870	1891
STIVERS, Hanna A.		1839	1898

70. Harrod Cemetery, Rebecca Bramlett, owner.
7 m. E of Bethlehem.

HARROD, Sarah	w. of D.	1814	1872
, Davis		1813	1862
, Barbara J.	d. of D. & S.	1854	1866

71. Thurman, Derner Cemetery.
5 m. S of Bethlehem.

DERNER, John		1858	
, Susie		1868	1918
THURMAN, John S.	s. of R. & E.	1880	1902
, Ransome		1850	
, Elizabeth		1852	1926

72. Scott Cemetery, -- Hayden, owner.
1 m. out Orem Lane.

SCOTT, Mildred G.
, Levi

73. Gill Graveyard.
2 m. SE of Pleasureville, near Elmburg.

BERGEN, Alpha	w. of C.	8- 6-1840	7-14-1870
GILL, John		1798	1852

74. Sanford Cemetery.
Half-way between New Castle and Lacey.

SANFORD, Chas. B.		7-15-1826	12-20-1854
, Martha	w. of C. B.		

75. Bruce Cemetery.
1 m. N of Hwy. 202, half-way between New Castle and Drennon.

BRUCE, Bettie			
, Jessie			
, Nannie	infant daughters of L. M. & E. J.	1854	1858

76. Logan Graveyard, E. C. Coleman, owner.
Hwy. 157 3 m. E of Sulphur.

LOGAN, John B.		1- 4-1804	9-24-1855
, Christiana	w. of J. B. 84th y.		1-29-1856

77. Martin Cemetery.
Hwy. 157, 3½ m. E of Sulphur.

COMBS, Lucy	w. of W. W.	2- 2-1819	1-19-1883
, Martha	d. of W. W. & N. M.	3- 5-1842	3-11-1844
CONSTANTINE, Eliza	w. of James	1-25-1813	2-13-1858
DEER, Elizabeth	w. of Larken	2-21-1805	11- 7-1860
MARTIN, Sarah	w. of Peter	4- 5-1785	1-20-1867
, Peter	b. Orange Co., Va.	1781	1- 1-1863
, Thos. Luther		1-28-1817	11-13-1853
SMITH, Fannie S.	d. of B. S. & F. G.	6-24-1860	10-22-1865

78. Defoe Graveyard.
½ m. S of Defoe on Hwy. 1922.

BAKER, Etta	w. of E. Vernon	1889	1913
BANTA, Lanny W.		1946	1969
BECKLEY, Jeff		1867	1943
, Emma		1883	1945
BISHOP, Wm. J.		1858	1932
, Sallie A.	his wife	1863	1938
BLACK, Mildred C.	w. of W. A.	1852	1914
, J. N.		1837	1909
BOHANNON, John L.		1879	1964
, Dick		1866	1941
, Joshua		1825	1907
CLARK, Mary Ellen	w. of Robt.	1867	1908
, John M.		1857	1931
, Mary Riner	his wife	1868	1947
DEAKINS, Sudie Johnson		1881	1936
, Robert H.		1951	
, Mary A.		1853	1939
DUNNAVENT, G. A.		1834	1908
ELLIS, John M.		1834	1900
, Irene	his wife	1832	1915
, Bunk		1863	
, Lora Elizabeth	w. of J. M.	1887	1910
ETHINGTON, J. N.		1861	1929

HENDERSON, John P.		1857	1914
HUDSON, A. M.		1849	1944
, Virginia		1865	1925
, Elvira		1843	1909
, Erastus		1844	1909
, Mary S.	his wife	1860	1918
JACKSON, John Hunt		1871	1948
, Amanda W.	his wife	1875	1923
LONG, Austin		1894	1968
, Mary E.	his wife	1906	1970
, Thomas		1856	1932
, Marietta	his wife	1857	1940
, Nick		1829	1909
, Prudence		1832	1902
, Nancy		1866	
MORRISON, J.	h. of Allene Hower	1887	1924
PENN, J. W.		1855	1923
, Eliza M.	his wife	1852	1929
RAISOR, Joshua		1848	1919
, Samuel			1918
RODGERS, Milton F.		1867	1939
RUCKER, James		1844	1912
, Elisha L.		1872	1936
, Lulu	his wife	1875	1958
, W. M.		1894	
, Susie	his wife	1894	1969
, Omer		1881	1955
, Susie A.		1861	1894
, Alveb		1864	1937
, Joe		1865	1962
, Mary I.	his wife	1883	1959
SHAW, Worth		1846	1927
, Mary Elizabeth	his wife	1855	1951
SCHUCK, John S.		6-16-1849	
, Sallie	his wife	2-14-1846	9- 7-1909
SNOW, Alvin F.	WW II	1917	1944
STIVERS, Nancy J.	w. of W. J.	1816	1900
, Bailey		1903	1951
, John		10-17-1835	12-15-1916
, Joe		1876	1942
, Annie B.	his wife	1873	1941
SUTHERLAND, Cora J.	w. of Garfield	1888	1918
THURMOND, Sallie B.	w. of Levi	1882	1911
TRUMAN, Armstead		1874	1935
, Wm. B.		1878	1956
, Levi		11-13-1876	5- 1-1967
, Clara E.	his wife	1877	1956
, Mary E.		1903	1971
WARD, Chester L.	WW I	1896	1966
, Ann		1898	1965
WAY, Mary Harlow		1885	1971
WHEELER, Lindon A.		1887	1952
, Mary T.	his wife	1887	1948

79. Hance - Wallace Graveyard.
½ m. up Six Mile Creek from Lockport.

ARNOLD, Hanna	w. of T. B.	5-12-1835	3- 9-1904
, T. B.		6-23-1827	6-11-1901
BURT, Andrew		12-25-1783	4-27-1858
HANCE, Anna Elizabeth		1900	1906
, Sidney		12- 1-1871	2-12-1903
, Bessie	his wife	8-27-1873	12- 2-1904
, Keturah	w. of John	4-26-1793	9-28-1838
HARROD, Wm.		3-31-1865	11- 3-1908
, Jennie		3-15-1871	
OLIVER, Nicholas		5-28-1790	7-15-1819
O'NAN, Sarah A.	w. of Wm.	1830	1855

OWEN, L. O.		1827	1892
POLLARD, Mary E.	w. of Frank m. 12-9-1875	8- 7-1858	5- 5-1885
, J. Leonard		1884	1905
ROWLETT, Frances E.	w. of J. M.	2- 8-1824	1- 3-1847
STIVERS, Mary E.	w. of W. R.	1856	1889
WALLACE, Benjamin		8-28-1803	10-27-1839
, John		7-16-1808	1-27-1858
, Joshua		7-31-1761	3- 1-1847
, Elizabeth	w. of J.	1789	1870

80. Logan Cemetery, E. C. Coleman, owner.
Hwy. 157, 3 m. E of Sulphur.

CHILTON, B. F.		1836	1927
LINDSEY, Dora	w. of James A.	5-17-1859	12- 9-1888
Perry, Sarah Olive	w. of E. K.	1855	1917
RANSDELL, Mary Ann	wife	1835	1920
, Joseph T.		10-15-1827	8-14-1856
, Notley	s. of Thos. J. & Polly	1837	1862
TURNER, J. B.		2-13-1803	11- 3-1898
, Martha A.		11-15-1822	4- 8-1850
, Caroline		2-12-1826	3-23-1900
, Frank		1859	1890
, T. J.		1848	1882

HENRY COUNTY CEMETERIES [KENTUCKY]

Part III

by

Willada Rickman Dent
(Mrs. Paul L. Dent)

South Pleasureville Public Cemetery
(Dutch Cemetery Company)

"The Highlands" Callaway Family Cemetery

Searching for markers at the Callaway Family Cemetery

(from left to right: Miss Frances Bate, Mr. J. Davis Marret, Mrs. Charles E. Craik, and Mrs. J. Davis Marret)

HENRY COUNTY CEMETERIES: PART III

By Mrs. Paul Dent*

81. South Pleasureville Public Cemetery (Dutch Cemetery Company)

Name	Note	Born	Died
ADAMS, W. B.		12-19-1827	12-17-1909
, Lucinda	w. of W. B. Adams	11-12-1829	4-14-1909
, J. G.		4-13-1830	5-27-1925
, Louisa V.		3- 7-1838	1-10-1903
, Annie T. Slemmons		11-27-1862	1-25-1896
, J. D.		1852	1934
, Luticia	w. of John Q. Adams	8-30-1834	2-19-1907
, Mary F.	w. of Joseph Adams	2- 2-1858	5-18-1903
, Clarence B.		9-18-1868	12-10-1900
, James R.		1858	No date
, Nancy C.	w. of James R. Adams	1861	1939
, F. B.		1861	1937
, Lula	(same marker as F. B. A.)	1862	1939
, Llewellyn		1903	1925
, Squire H.		1862	1934
, Mary Tinie	(same marker as S. H. A.)	1865	1926
, David E.		9-26-1887	10-30-1953
, Audrey		5-11-1886	4-28-1957
, John J.		1864	1934
, Fannie W.		1868	1953
, Harry		1894	1931
, Eva Lou		1896	1924
, Jesse T.		1900	1924
, Helen T.	aged 2 mos.	No dates	
, Mary A.	w. of H. M. Adams	9-21-1882	1-14-1915
, Squire		1874	1962
, Mattie M.	(same marker as S. A.)	1871	1947
, Sara E.	d. of S. and M. Adams	12-12-1910	5- 2-1930
, C. W.		Illegible	1904
, C. B., M.D.		1861	1895
, Renie B. McGowan		1870	1938
, Charlie Blanche		1895	1912
, Henry S.		1874	1964
, Cordia		1885	1963
, Arthur R.	W.W. I.	10- 6-1892	8-21-1962
, W. M.		1882	1960
, Mary E.	same marker as W. M. A.	1889	No date
, George M.		1862	1951
, Annie C.	w. of George M. A.	1868	1919
, Mabel	w. of George M. A.	1891	1947
, Carl B.		1894	1922
, Delbert H.		1898	1963
, Dorothy R.	same marker as D. H. A.	1903	No date
, Virgil		6-16-1899	9- 2-1974
, Marietta A.		6-14-1903	10-12-1976
, Ernest A.		1869	No date
, Florence Caplinger		1872	No date
ADCOCK, Carroll		1867	19__
, Nora	same marker as C. A.	1869	19__
ADLER, A. G.		1-17-1847	1-19-1929
, Ollie Johnson	w. of A. G. A.	11-23-1848	9-29-1918
, Eliza Bell		4-20-1876	12-20-1910
, Eddie		1897	No date
, Anna	same marker as E. A.	1900	1940
, Robert E.		1892	1954
, Mary E.	same marker as R. E. A.	1895	19__
, Blaine		1896	No date
, Gladys K.	same marker as B. A.	1900	No date
, Virginia		No date	No date
, Rhonda Sue		1965	1966

*MRS. PAUL DENT, Louisville, is an active Filsonian and local historian.

ALDRIDGE, William		1854	1923
, Louise	same marker as W. A.	1869	1943
, John J.		12-15-1895	5- 2-1976
, Corinne	same marker as J. J. A.	11- 7-1902	No date
ALEXANDER-BOTTOM-PORTER family marker			
, Arthur Alexander		1853	1930
, Sibbie B. Alexander		1855	1919
, Cora Alexander		1882	1968
ALISON , Virgil		1881	1953
(ALLISON), Effie W.		1885	1943
, Paul		1906	1924
AMBROSE, William L.		1872	1940
, Isa Lena H.		1890	1973
ANDERSON, James S.		1888	1971
, Laura E.	(same marker as J. S. A.)	1896	19__
Frank P.	"Father"	1889	1969
, Hazel R.	"Mother" (same marker as F. P. A.)	1888	1949
ANNIS, Willie Francis	Pvt. 1 Co 159 Ky W.W. I.	10-31-1889	9-16-1971
ARNOLD, Wilson W.	"Father"	1869	1938
, Oda	"Mother" w. of W. W. A.	1874	1949
, Curtis M.		1893	1970
, Lorena		1897	1931
, Rose V.		1910	No date
, Lillian		1921	1924
, Sidney		1892	1970
, Bertha R.	(same marker as S. A.)	1898	19__
, Ralph B.	PFC U.S.A. Ky W.W. II	1-29-1926	10- 5-1968
, Dolly B.	(same marker as R. B. A.)	1929	1972
, David		2- 5-1950	1950
ARNSPARGER, M.		1851	1918
, Ida M.		1858	1926
, Sarah Elizabeth		1881	1965
, William E.	"Father"	9-13-1866	9- 5-1891
, Birdie	d. of Haden and Bettie A.	11-10-1880	8-28-1884
, Arthur H.		1883	1958
, Nancy G.		1886	1962
, Ernest		1869	1921
, Florence Caplinger		1872	1946
, Lora Knight		1893	1976
, Clifton		1901	No date
, Eva McGowan		1909	No date
, Marion		1910	No date
ASHBY, A. J.		1865	1956
, Sallie	(same marker as A. J. A.)	1878	1959
ASHLEY, John		1879	1971
, Dell	(same marker as J. A.)	1879	1957
ATCHINSON, Elmer		1892	No date
, Clara B. Terrell	(same marker as E. A.)	1899	No date
AYNES, Samuel		1855	1929
, Margaret		1861	1948
, Fountain S.		1-24-1878	3-11-1963
, J. N.	family marker	9-17-1860	2-12-1935
, Mattie	(same marker as J. N. A.)	5- 5-1864	7-28-1909
, Carrie H.	(same marker as J. N. A.)	2-15-1883	4-10-1936
, Orvil	(same marker as J. N. A.)	7- 4-1891	No date
, Harvey M.	(same marker as J. N. A.)	3-27-1894	No date
, Lilian	(same marker as J. N. A.)	5-22-1897	No date
, Delbert	(same marker as J. N. A.)	10-10-1900	4-21-1904
, James		6-27-1881	12-18-1938
, Nellie A.		2-24-1892	7-15-1893
, Haschal H.	(same marker as Nellie)	9-10-1899	12- 5-1901
, Sallie Bowling		9- 4-1883	12-14-1973
, Ollie James		1899	1929
, Sylvan		1897	1964
, Elmer		1895	No date
, Mary Demaree	(same marker as Elmer)	1893	1964
BABBITT, Willis	"Father"	1878	1945
, Georgia H.	"Mother"	1888	1977
BAIN, Ira Goethe		12-16-1874	11- 3-1962
, Lucy Johnson		3-28-1872	10-26-1956

Name		Remarks	Born	Died
BAKER,	Rev. A. W.		11-11-1830	11-28-1892
	, Melinda		2- 5-1829	No date
	, Louisa	w. of A. W. B.	10-10-1857	3-31-1885
	, Louisa	d. of A. W. B.	3-30-1885	6-15-1885
	, George Thomas		1856	1895
	, Idabell	(same marker as G. T. B.)	1866	1911
	, Issac E.		1871	1938
	, Mamie E.	(same marker as I. E. B.)	1860	No date
	, James A.		11-15-1851	10-14-1892
	, Callie M.		6- 6-1876	3- 6-1892
	, Lonzo S.		1865	1946
	, Nannie	(same marker as L. S. B.)	1865	1946
	, Ralph			1913
	, Isaac	(same marker as Ralph B.)	1903	1910
	, Henrietta T.		10- 8-1901	No date
	, Edna Smith		1875	1944
	, Maurice		1895	1919
	, Walker		1856	1928
	, Lovie P.	(same marker as Walker B.)	1873	1948
	, Anne M.	w. of Curtis B.	1898	1960
	, Curtis		2-16-1904	2-29-1968
	, Harvey Webster		No date	No date
	, William H.		1- 8-1910	7- 5-1964
	, Ethel Gill		12- 5-1910	No date
	, William Earl		10- 6-1930	11-11-1949
	, James V.		1933	1965
	, Linda Laverne		No date	1-12-1948
	, James V. Jr.		No date	No date
BANTA,	Peter	aged 68 yrs. 10 mos. 17 das.		4-23-1832
	, Isaac		7-27-1809	5- 2-1881
	, Cassandra R.	w. of Isaac B.	12-12-1812	11-4-1880
	, Lucy Jane	w. of B. T. Banta and d. of W. H. and C. Quisenberry aged 27 yrs.		9- 5-1885
	, Samuel I.	s. of W. C. and Laura B.	3-10-1885	5-31-1885
	, Mary T.	d. of W. C. and Laura B.	6- 5-1900	1- 5-1902
	, Cassie	d. of W. C. and Laura B.	3-26-1892	10- 3-1895
	, Edgar	s. of W. C. and Laura B.	9-17-1902	2-27-1903
	, H. G.	"Father"	4-14-1821	12-22-1877
	, Bettie	"Mother" (same marker as H. G. B.)	10-30-1825	10- 9-1907
	, W. H.		1843	1862
	, A. W.		2-22-1832	No date
	, Sarah E.	w. of A. W. (same marker)	12- 7-1833	10- 3-1900
	, Edward		1870	1929
	, Margaret I.		1870	1952
	, W. D.		12-10-18__	8-16-1914
	, Anna	w. of W. D. (same marker)	2-28-1840	5- 2-1914
	, Virgil A.		1877	1954
	, Ralph	"Father"	1899	1950
	, M. Grace Jones	"Mother"	1894	1939
	, I. W.	"Pappy"	3-12-1849	4-14-1923
	,	"Mammy" (No given name)	2- 2-1849	11-11-1933
	, Claude A.		1873	1953
	, Elsey C.		1877	1892
	, Willie C.		1859	1936
	, Carrie T.		1860	1931
	, Lev J.		5-28-1865	9- 7-1957
	, Emma Perry		No date	12-30-1958
	, Grace Clayton		No date	No date
	, Octavus Newton		1866	1899
	, Minnie Hower		1872	1959
	, John M.		1872	1911
	, Virginia		1909	1916
	, William L.		1876	1948
	, Griffin Drane		1847	1912
	, Melissa Tucker		1850	1929
	, Minnie H.		1881	1964
	, Flora Roberts	"Mother"	4- 6-1885	5- 5-1966
	, Stephen W.		1892	1965
	, Boyd M.		1893	1977
	, Lula E.	(same marker as Boyd M. B.)	1903	1971

Name	Remarks	Born	Died
, Vachel G. Sr.		1903	1949
, Virginia B.	(same marker as Vachel B. Sr.)	1902	1954
BARNES, David	(same marker as Lowenback)	11-26-1820	6-15-1904
, George R.		1955	1973
, Louise		No date	10- 4-1956
BARNSFATHER, James S.		2-12-1896	2-19-1968
, Rena B.	(same marker as Jas. S. B.)	6- 4-1899	No date
BARTON, George W.		10-18-1839	7-24-1905
, Marium Graham	w. of G. W. B.	1- 4-1839	1-30-1890
, Willie S.	s. of Ballard and Hallie	4-19-1895	7- 8-1898
, Willie		4-18-1861	10-18-1901
, Sybel	(same marker as Willie B.)	1862	1944
, Leonard		1864	1929
, Annie	(same marker as Leonard B.)	1868	1944
BATES, Teeny	(Shannon family marker)	1928	1949
BATTERTON, Tyra	"Father" aged 77yrs.		9- 7-1897
, Elizabeth	"Mother" aged 54yrs.		1-16-1897
, W. T.	s. of E. and L. Shuck (Batterton marker)		No dates
, James M.		3-24-1857	5-11-1928
, Emily H.		3-16-1859	11- 5-1880
, Katie R.		10-24-1866	9-10-1908
, Levia Ann		5-11-1875	12-10-1940
, Mary James		1893	1927
, Eddie T.	(Batterton-Robertson marker)	1891	1976
, Mabel R.	(same marker as Eddie T. B.)	1895	No date
, Troy Hillis	(Vietnam)	10-19-1948	4- 8-1970
BATTS, J. M.		12-28-1854	11-11-1931
, Martha J.		11-12-1853	3-13-1931
, Mattie	(Batts-Scobee marker)	2-12-1879	2-16-1942
BAUGH, George T.		8-10-1870	5-18-1944
, Laura S.	(same marker as Geo. T. B.)	10-11-1872	3- 4-1963
BAXTER, Celester		1900	No date
, Alma		1904	No date
, R. C.		1935	1952
BEARD, Roy Ansel		1880	1903
, Willis Banta		1885	1902
, Warren Foree	s. of Dr. E. F. and J. L. Beard	5-22-1887	3- 9-1889
BECKLEY, S. T.		1846	1925
, Ella O.	(same marker as S. T. B.)	1850	1924
, Harry R.		1885	1975
, Ethel M.	(same marker as Harry R. B.)	1892	1974
, Dorothy	"Mother of Brenda, Pam and Glen"	1929	1953
BEESON, F. Lucille	"Mother of Avis Willis and Darius Hankins 1917"		No dates
BELL, Isafena	w. of John H. Bell	6-28-1819	7-21-1885
, John H.		1862	1932
, Nancy Jane	(same marker as John H. Bell)	1865	1949
, Matie May	d. of J. H. and Nancy Bell	3-13-1893	11-22-1894
, William T.		1869	1931
, Mary L.	(same marker as Wm. T. Bell)	1865	1960
BELWOOD, Eugene		1860	1930
, Laura H.	(same stone as Eugene B.)	1860	1927
, Robert Burns	"Father"	1888	1969
, Mattie Mitchell	"Mother" (same marker as R. B. B.)	1889	1951
BENNETT, Robert		1890	1961
, Lula M.		1893	1961
, Guy H.		1899	1967
, Katherine L.		1900	No date
BERGEN, George		9- 2-1786	10-10-1869
, Magdalena	w. of Geo. B.	11-21-1787	4- 1-1854
, John		5-26-1816	4-23-1852
, Albert	aged 15yrs. 9mos. 21das.		7-13-1841
, Mildred	w. of Geo. B.	11-20-1798	3-20-1869
, Jacob		8- 1-1801	1-24-1863
, Sallie	"My Mother"	5-15-1807	9-26-1862
, John T.		7-16-1840	5-11-1862
, Albert		9-20-1820	9-10-1893
, Mary J.	w. of A. B.	6-20-1819	6-10-1899
, George W.		2-15-1844	12- 2-1872
(small marker illegible)			
, Albert Newton		1851	1932
, Flora Moore	(same marker as Albert N. B.)	1854	1933

Name	Note	Born	Died
, Robert G.		1858	1903
, (B. E.?)		4-21-1861	9- 8-1906
, Carrie Smith		2-28-1863	12-19-1950
, Beth Frances	d. of B. E. and Carrie B.)	1904	1906
, Lee Roy		No dates given	
, George Albert		10-31-1871	8- 2-1955
BEVERLY-BRUCE (family marker)			
, Willie D.		1888	No date
, Carrie D.	(same marker as Willie D. B.)	1892	No date
, Leona		1928	1939
, Charles A.		1899	No date
, Anna A.		1899	1937
, Verdella C.	wife	1907	1975
, Stephen B.		1858	1929
, Elizabeth Florence		1870	1964
, Marvin		1901	No date
, Lucille	(same marker as Marvin B.)	1905	No date
, Russell H.		12-15-1951	10-11-1973
, Joan		1873	1952
BERNHARDT, Myrtle B.	(same marker as I. M. Stephens)	1865	1941
BERRY, Robert L.		1870	1926
, Nora		1874	1944
, Charles		1897	No date
, Lillian Burgin		1898	1965
BEUTEL, Rachel E.	"Mother"	1843	1921
, John		4- 7-1874	5- 2-1951
, Fred T.	married Clemma G. 4-3-1916	1-29-1897	No date
, Clemma G.	(same marker as Fred T. B.)	6-22-1898	12-21-1975
, Charles		1865	1926
, Sallie	(same marker as Charles B.)	1862	1940
, Herbert A.		6- 1-1892	8-31-1977
, Carrie E.		3-26-1894	No date
BIBB, Elizabeth Claxon		1846	1927
, W. E.		1869	1911
, Ella	w. of W. E. B. (same marker as W. E. B.)	1865	1933
, William A.		7-27-1848	5-26-1908
, Caroline		8- 4-1855	2-26-1906
, Whitley		1880	1967
, Susie	(same marker as Whitley B.)	1879	1974
, Mary Katherine	"Sister"	1878	1938
, Melvira Bibb Thomas		1882	1963
BIBB-GIVIDAN (family marker)			
BIBB, Frank E. Bibb		9-28-1884	8- 6-1949
, Ella M.		9-10-1888	2-10-1975
BICKERS, Charles W.		1893	1974
, Emma L.	(same marker as Charles W. B.)	1894	No date
BIERMAN, Edward A.		1885	1958
, Elizabeth B.	(same marker as Edward A. B.)	1888	1977
BIRCHETT-O'NAN-SPENCER (family marker)			
, John C. Birchett		1862	1925
, Maria Birchett Maddox		1856	1940
, Harry		2-14-1879	6- 2-1955
, Viola Maud Mays		10-27-1878	8- 3-1963
BIRCHETT-O'NAN (family marker)			
, Earl R. O'Nan		1882	1907
, Jerome G. Birchett		1890	1908
, William Maddox		8-22-1875	10-25-1959
, Theodosia Bedford		11-14-1886	8-24-1964
BIRD, G. Caldwell	W.W. I	9-19-1889	2-26-1972
BLACK, Elzy B.		1-29-1837	10-19-1917
, Mary S.	w. of Elzy Black	12-27-1839	11- 2-1894
, Lena Banta		5-30-1869	6-27-1960
, Herman		3-30-1885	9-27-1959
, Thomas N.		6-14-1879	8-14-1957
, Minnie B.		5-27-1879	11-22-1972
, Infant	daughter of T M. and M. M. B.		2-20-1915
, G. T.		1851	1930
, Melina		1855	1938
, Elmer		1878	1933
, Clara Bush		1884	1947
, Lindsay		1891	1894

, Mary E.		1888	1893
, Arthur		1881	1938
BLACKABY, Humphrey		4-11-1877	No date
, Minnie	(same marker as Humphrey)	1- 7-1882	6-28-1959
, Clara Douthett		1880	1945
, Lemuel T.		1882	1962
, Hallie D.	(same marker as Lemuel)	1892	1950
, Orland		1889	1962
, Katie R.	(same marker as Orland)	1897	1963
, Arthur		1887	1947
, Elizabeth M.	(same marker as Arthur)	1893	1942
, Jessie Kelley		1905	1927
, Laura T.		1897	1961
BLACKWELL, J. S.		1844	1915
, Marticia	w. of J. S. B.	8- 8-1846	5-30-1879
, Eliza	w. of J. S. B.	5-16-1856	8-11-1881
, Callard	s. of J. S. and Eliza B.	8- 8-1881	8-11-1881
, Melissa	w. of J. S. B.	2-14-1858	7- 2-1911
, Clemmye W.		1879	1935
, Nellie	w. of S. C. B.	4-11-1870	8- 5-1890
BLAND, Curtis L.	"Father"	2-28-1881	2-27-1970
BOGGS, Elizabeth Garrett	"My Mother"	6-13-1809	7- 6-1885
BOHANNON, Henry		9-22-1818	5- 3-1898
, Permelia	w. of Henry	1828	No date
(On same marker as Henry and Permelia)			
, I. S.		1860	1948
, V. B.		1866	1937
, W. J.		1885	1895
, I. L.		1893	1895
, N. M.		1896	1917
, L. E.		1898	1920
, E. V.		1909	1910
, A. B.		1907	1907
, Nathaniel	"Husband"	10-22-1887	7-10-1911
, Katie Wylie	"Wife"	1890	1956
, John H.	"Father"	1859	1931
, Callie Moss	"Mother"	1864	1932
, Bertha May	"Daughter"	1898	1914
(John H., Callie Moss and Bertha on same marker)			
, Infant	son of H. H. and Callie B.	1-22-1891	1-22-1891
, Mary Jane	w. of John B.	5- 5-1858	3- 4-1885
, Russell C.	Ky Pvt. U.S. Army W.W. II	5- 2-1914	1-18-1972
, Dwayne		No date	4-30-1962
, J. M.		1886	No date
, Jennie Wylie	(same marker as J. M. B.)	1887	1964
, David S.	s. of J. M. and J. W. B.	8-23-1912	4-18-1913
BONDURANT, James		12-10-1872	1- 4-1930
, Nannie		3- 6-1876	1-16-1960
, Arthur		1877	1935
, William O.		10- 5-1879	8- 9-1952
BOOTH, Mark L.		1859	1935
, Alice A.		1879	1946
, Rosa Jennings	"Mother"	1894	1946
, Robert E.	"Father"	1893	1973
, Carrie Violet	"Mother"	1896	1976
BOTTOM-ALEXANDER-PORTER family marker			
, Samuel M. Bottom		1870	1950
, Willie A. Bottom		1888	1972
BOULWARE, Mary J.		12-25-1841	12-16-1918
, Robert Thomas		1906	1952
, H. Augusta		1883	1927
, J. Thomas		1884	1930
BOYD, J. D.		No date	No date
, Fannie		1864	1926
BRADLEY, James P.	Spanish American War	2-23-1874	6-26-1950
, Essie B.	(same marker as James P. B.)	1884	1939
, Lieut. J. M.	Co I 13 Ky. Inf.		No dates
, Mary Elizabeth	w. of J. M. B.	5-14-1848	12-30-1890
BRADSHAW, Ella Lee	w. of C. T. Bradshaw	11-20-1865	4-22-1889
, Preston Lee	s. of C. T. and Ella L. B.	11- 6-1887	2- 9-1890
BRAMBLETT, William F.		1879	1963

Name	Remarks	Birth	Death
, Rebecca D.		1895	No date
, Claud	"Son"	1899	1975
, J. Melton		1899	1971
, Shirley	(same marker as J. Melton B.)	1909	No date
BRANAMAN, Salem W.		2-16-1822	8-31-1902
, Mary B.	w. of Salem B. (same marker)	1837	1924
, William S.		6-12-1868	3-24-1909
, Sallie		8-25-1861	4-10-1941
, Baby		1-16-1900	1900
, Roger	TEC4. Signal Corp W.W. II	11-24-1897	5-26-1962
BRASHEAR, James T.		1850	1924
BRAWNER, Mary D.	w. of G. W. B.	4- 9-1857	8-15-1876
, Infant	d. of G. W. and M. D. B.	8-13-1876	8-14-1876
, Levia		2- 9-1878	5-21-1954
, Robert F.	(same marker as Levia)	3-10-1875	11-16-1954
, Harvie		7-16-1876	7-25-1897
, Garrye		1879	1922
BRECKINRIDGE, Catherine	"Mother"	1827	9- 3-1893
BRIGHT, Taylor		1887	1970
, Ethel Gordon		1893	1940
, William M.		8- 2-1878	No date
, Birdie A.		10-30-1881	5-18-1960
, Infant	s. of Wm. and B. B.		1916
BROOKS, Wiley C.		2-20-1876	1- 3-1959
, Missouri Clark	"Mother"	1-22-1893	7-10-1972
BROUGHTON, Latha		11- 4-1890	8-11-1970
, Pearl W.		11-18-1893	5- 5-1969
, Fielding D.		1895	No date
, Mattie D.		1898	1966
BROWN, Walter S.	"Father"	1859	1924
, Anna S.	"Mother"	1865	1940
, Minerva A.		1835	1912
, Enoch M.		1825	1910
, Tilden H.	"Father"	1876	1954
, Cleo Thomas	"Mother"	1884	1975
, Irene T.	"Daughter"	1905	1951
, David		1877	1947
, Iva E.		1883	1974
, John M.	Pvt. 3 Ky. Inf.	3-30-1867	2- 3-1942
, Sallie Smoot		5-15-1878	9- 1-1951
, Leonard R.	Knight-Brown-Watkins marker	1879	1955
, Clara K.	Knight-Brown-Watkins marker	1882	1955
, Myrtle		1901	No date
BROWNING, Samuel J. T.		1876	1958
, Emma		5-14-1884	11-15-1970
BROWN, Bullock B.	"Father"	1853	1918
, Sarah M.	"Mother" w. of Bullock B.	1857	1915
BRUCE, Charles		1876	1949
, Emma B.		1877	1936
, E. I.		1909	1955
, Evelyn A.		1910	1971
BRYANT, Henrietta	"Mother"	1843	1921
, James P.		9- 9-1853	11-28-1903
, Lena W.		4-17-1862	10-28-1945
, Asa Tucker		1876	1941
, Frances Kesler	(same marker as Asa B.)	No date	No date
, Lorina Margaret		1906	1968
, Walker	s. of W. B. and Mary Snook B.	1902	1905
BUFORD, Thomas L.	(Hall-Buford family marker)	1850	1917
, Rebecca Jane Hall	w. of Thos. L. B.	1862	1901
, Vida T.		1876	1924
, James Paul		1904	1927
, Marjorie T.		1906	1923
BURNETT, Marticia Bergen		5- 2-1862	2- 2-1955
BUSH, E. T.		5-13-1834	1- 5-1932
, Mary		12-11-1846	8-29-1916
, Anderson		1-11-1865	10-24-1931
, James P.		1874	1952
, Edmund S.		9-16-1869	1-27-1916
, Ida Mae	w. of Edmund S. B.	3-31-1877	2-12-1899
, "Our Baby"	(same marker as E. S. & I. M. B.) aged 9das.		1-31-1899

Name	Remarks	Born	Died
, James L.		1851	1941
, America F.	(same marker as Jas. L. B.)	1856	1941
, Mat	"Father"	6- 7-1859	1- 4-1914
, Louisa Crawford	"Mother" w. of Mat B.	9-14-1858	8-24-1910
, Ida C.	(same marker as Mat B.)	1- 3-1880	No date
, Corda W.		7- 1-1886	No date
, Maude	(same marker as Mat B.)	4-28-1892	1928
, Rena	(same marker as Mat B.)	6- 4-1898	No date
, Manard S.	"Father"	1872	1950
, Nora B.	"Mother" (same marker as M. S. B.)	1878	1928
, Margaret		1906	1950
, Guthrie N.	W.W.	7- 6-1908	1-28-1975
, C. Reese		10-25-1892	12-29-1972
, Ida Roberts	(same marker as I. R. B.)	4-17-1894	12-29-1972
BYERS, William		1846	1918
, Sarah	(same marker as Wm. B.)	1852	1935
, Ernest		11- 3-1880	3-11-1962
, Willie		1877	1956
, Reed Clayton		1872	1930
, Evelyn Wilhite	(same marker as R. C. B.)	1879	1921
, Flora Lucille		1916	No date
, Mable Sewell		1892	1925
, Orville		1886	1972
, Will Allen		1914	1944
, Howard S.		1875	1952
, Josie E.	(same marker as H. S. B.)	1875	1946
CAIN, John W.		1858	No date
, Ellen	(same marker as John W. C.)	1864	No date
, Lelia		1887	1948
, N. Colby		1886	1959
, Maude M.	(same marker as N. Colby C.)	1908	1959
CALDWELL, R. C.		1899	No date
, Anna Belle		1903	1973
CALVERT, Ruth Flood		1903	1933
, Lurline Fallis		1891	No date
CAPLINGER, William T.	"Husband"	1875	1938
, Maud V.	"Wife"	1879	1959
, Jacob B.	"Father"	1843	1913
Charity E.	"Mother"	1845	1926
CARTER, Joseph		1847	1924
, Maria Alva	w. of Jos. C. (same marker)	1852	19__
, Jordan Witt		1- 3-1876	7- 6-1943
, Mary Yankey		2-12-1885	5- 9-1964
, Elizabeth M. Witt		10-29-1868	3-31-1926
, Joseph D. Sr.		1892	1967
, Charles Hicks		4-13-1911	4-29-1937
, Joseph D.		11- 3-1913	5- 9-1960
, Linden		6-30-1889	3-27-1968
, Frances	w. of L. C.	1891	1962
, Ira		1882	1949
, Ollie		1887	1967
, James C.		11-20-1945	5-31-1958
CASEY-HENDERSON family marker			
, Walter L.		1897	1976
, Lepla Henderson		1897	1963
, Donald R.		1919	1947
CAYUGA,		illegible	illegible
CHADWELL, Ova	'Father"	11-14-1879	1-24-1936
, Ida B.	"Mother"	1880	1959
, Hessie Chadwell Floyd	"Daughter"	1907	1943
, James D.		1898	1972
, Jane W.	(same marker as Jas. D. C.)	1906	No date
CHILTON, Margaret	w. of N. P. Chilton	1-29-1836	1-16-1901
, Della W.	w. of N. P. Chilton	12-14-1881	2-24-1919
, David		1873	1944
, Hattie		1871	1935
CHISHOLM, Jim		7-16-1891	6- 4-1937
, Ida		1892	No date
, Eddie T.	Ky. Pvt Co D 128 Inf. W.W. I	12- 2-1895	2-28-1962
, Carrie M. Lee	(same marker as Eddie T. C.)	1912	No date

Name	Remarks	Born	Died
CLARK, Mathew		5- 5-1808	5-27-1886
CLARKE, C.		1846	1926
, Sarah E.	(same marker as C. C.)	1854	1940
, James		1817	1882
, J. S.	Masonic Emblem on marker	12-28-1816	12- 3-1876
, Mary J.	d. of J. S. and E. W. Clarke	1-26-1843	12- 8-1870
, Arthur		2-25-1878	12-17-1964
CLARK or CLARKE, W. R.		1849	1926
, Annie M.	w. of W. R. C. (same marker)	1863	1928
, Walter V.		3- 1-1893	No date
, Ella P.		2-27-1899	8- 9-1973
, Squire E.		4-18-1882	1-22-1957
, Lena		11-20-1892	2-20-1960
CLAXON, Spencer		7-28-1827	5-10-1885
, John W.		11- 8-1858	1-13-1905
, Lydia	(same marker as John W. C.)	illegible	illegible
, John Keen	(same marker as John W. C.)	illegible	illegible
, Tinie	w. of Spencer Claxon	3- 2-1836	12-29-1876
, Mary Claxon Jessee	w. of J. F. Jessee	4- 8-1867	11-13-1896
, Ella Morriss Claxon		1883	1964
CLAYTON, Joseph D.		6- 6-1886	4-30-1966
, Hallie K.		8-10-1890	10-25-1974
CLEMENTS, J. W.	"Father"	1-28-1830	No date
, M. L.	"Mother"	4-18-1834	8-22-1896
, Children of J. W. and M. L. C.: J. W.; L. S.; K. S.; W. O.; Daughter A B.; S. E.; E. F.; M. E.; M. L.; F. A.		No dates on marker	
, Naomi	w. of J. T. C.	3-18-1873	10-27-1900
, W. O.	"Brother"	1-18-1878	3-29-1906
, Hugh	Spanish American War		No dates
, Ruth		5-18-1883	12-18-1972
, Sue Cubbage		1879	1967
, R. J.		7- 3-1835	12-18-1910
, Sallie	"Mother"	3-19-1835	3-25-1902
, James		1846	1926
, Mary		1846	1936
, Anna Clements Hughes		1878	1943
, Amster B.		1857	1923
, Mary E.	(same marker as A. B. C.)	1860	1927
, Charles Sanford		8- 8-1897	12-30-1966
, Jake A.		3-17-1878	5-28-1964
, Mary W.	(same marker as Jake A. C.)	3-10-1889	12-27-1967
, Sidney R., Sr.		1895	No date
, Blanche Pate	(same marker as Sidney R. C., Sr.)	1901	1959
, Linda Sue	d. of Sidney and Martha C.	No date	10-17-1959
, William	husb. of Addie McDaniel	10-30-1888	19__
, Addie McDaniel	(same marker as Wm. C.)	8-10-1892	5-17-1933
, Corrine		9-17-1899	12-30-1966
CLEVELAND, Horace S.		3-18-1899	No date
, Williebel Chilton		1- 9-1900	7-19-1975
CLUBB, Joel H.		1- 2-1815	1- 4-1884
, Elizabeth Ann	w. of Joel H. C.	8-21-1815	9-24-1894
, Prentis		11-18-1857	4-16-1924
, Annie Booth		12-31-1861	7-12-1950
, Burlington		7-23-1842	12-28-1919
, Sarah E.	(same marker as B. C.)	5- 7-1846	4-23-1906
, C. C.		1- 4-1846	9- 5-1905
, Matilda	w. of C. C. C.	12-22-1847	2-19-1889
, B. H.		1841	1926
, Sallie	w. of B. H. C.	1857	1910
, H. P.		1855	1935
, Mary E.	w. of H. P. C. (same marker)	1849	1922
, F. L.		1853	1933
, Sarah C.	w. of F. L. C.	1850	1922
, Kossuth		1851	1935
, Judith	(same marker as K. C.)	1857	1923
, Burke	(same marker as K. C. and J. C.)	1881	1896
, John W., M.D.		4-27-1860	6-30-1941
, Elizabeth D.	w. of J. W. C. (same marker)	10-18-1872	1-29-1949
, Boyd W.		5-25-1883	6-27-1950
, E. Fay		7- 5-1889	No date

Name	Note	Born	Died
, Elzy		9-27-1865	12- 3-1954
, Addie Jacoby	(same marker as Elzy C.)	2- 6-1887	No date
, Claude		1870	1936
, Nora	w. of Claude C.	3-16-1872	7- 8-1898
, "Our Baby"			No date
, Lillian L. Holland		1- 8-1873	8-10-1953
, Clarence M.		1864	1943
, Donna May		1868	1930
, Curtis C.		1868	1939
, Mattie E.	,same marker as Curtis C. C.)	1870	1952
, Fannie B.	w. of W. P. C.	4-25-1872	3-19-1898
, Harry		1866	1957
, Virgie	w. of Harry C. (same marker)	7-19-1870	4-20-1897
, Virginia Dudley	w. of Harry C. (same marker)	1872	1967
, Joel Perry		1906	1956
, Charlsie Lancaster	w. of Joel Perry C.	1912	No date
, Mary Isabel Clubb Wood		3-29-1897	4-16-1964
, Lena	w. of H. M. C.	4-20-1872	2- 8-1909
, Marshall		10-29-1888	4-10-1928
, Francis		1902	1921
, George C.		1919	No date
, Catherine M.	(same marker as Geo. C. C.)	1919	1967
COALMAN, J. D.	"Father"	7-14-1851	11- 7-1902
, M. E.	"Mother" (same marker as J. D. C.)	8- 7-1853	1-26-1927
COCKRELL, Will		9-27-1876	8- 7-1937
, Fannie	(same marker as Will C.)	4- 8-1889	8-19-1964
, Vera Simmons	(same marker as Will C.)	5- 8-1910	4-24-1931
COFER and , Linden Perry Cofer	W.W. I.	4-14-1899	11-24-1954
MEFFORD , Sadie M.	(Medford-Cofer family marker)	7-13-1905	No date
, Linden Stanley		11-20-1921	2-27-1922
COLLETT, Henry C.		12-19-1882	8-24-1950
, Nannie B.	(same marker as Henry C. C.)	1885	1958
, Judy Ann			5-16-1953
COLLINS, John William		1878	1938
, Flora Wilhite	w. of John Wm. C.	1885	1965
COOK, William P.		1878	1935
, Mary Belle	w. of Wm. P. C. (same marker)	1885	No date
, Willie M.		1886	1913
, Hallie R.	w. of W. M. C.	1888	No date
, Aneita B.	d. of Wm. M. and H. R. C.		No date
COOPPER-WADE, Sarah A.	(family marker)	12-13-1826	11- 7-1846
, Mary J.	aged 74yrs		4-29-1903
, Rebecca		4-23-1830	2-20-1865
COOTS, Wilson P.		6-20-1818	7-30-1900
, Celia K.	(same marker as Wilson P. C.)	5- 2-1839	11-10-1900
COPPERSMITH, Lloyd		1899	1975
, Essie		1902	No date
COUNTS, Rev. Gilbert E.		1893	1965
, Ellen Roberts		1907	No date
, Raymond		1907	No date
, Helen R.		1900	No date
COX, John		1853	1922
, Bettie		1860	1928
, James Marion		1889	1942
, S. Leonard		1889	1941
, Susan Frost	w. of Mat Cox	1883	1972
, Oscar		10-25-1892	3- 6-1976
, Ida K.	(same marker as Oscar Cox)	11-17-1892	No date
, Earl		8-12-1899	9-15-1976
, Goldie Keenan	(same marker as Earl Cox)	2-14-1898	1- 3-1975
, James M.		1873	1952
, Mary	(same marker as James M. Cox)	1872	1946
, James H.	"Our Son"	5-27-1909	3- 1-1930
, A. D.		1876	1947
, Lula	(same marker as A. D. Cox)	1883	1943
CRAIG, Thomas J.		9- 4-1880	2-10-1962
, George		11-27-1890	11-10-1958
, Leva		7- 7-1899	8-14-1956
CRAIGMYLE, Lindsey		1872	1963
, Ida Simpson	(same marker as Lindsey C.)	1873	1958
CRAIGMYLES, J. T. "Deter"		9- 6-1897	No date

Name	Remarks	Born	Died
	Married 9-14-1918 (same marker)		
, Hallie Floyd		6-24-1898	No date
CRAWFORD, John		5- 1-1881	7- 2-1947
, Betsy		1889	1964
CRUTCHER, George T.	"Father"	1889	1961
, Jeanetta	"Mother"	1882	1949
, Ruth Crutcher Gordod	"Sister"	1906	1959
, Hattie S.	"Mother"	1881	1961
, Robert Thomas Crutcher		9-28-1904	3-19-1910
CUBB, George T.		1842	1917
, Catherine	(same marker as George T. C.)	1843	1922
CUBBAGE, Ben W.		1882	1936
, Marie Saells		1885	1971
, Hieatt C.		1906	1931
, Forest W.		1871	1962
, America		1875	1958
CURTRIGHT, H. K.		1870	1936
, Sarah D.		1872	1951
, Henry Herndon		1901	1967
DARNOLD, Richard		9- 5-1833	3-10-1893
, Sarah	"Mother"	4- 6-1831	3- 2-1898
, Eugene	(same marker as Margaret R. D.)	6-24-1857	No date
, Margaret D. Riner	w. of Eugene D.	6-25-1857	12-30-1918
, J. B.		5-20-1882	8- 4-1908
, Obed W.		3-22-1863	7-19-1908
DAVIS, J. Slater		1876	1956
, Bertie Hall	(same marker as J. Slater D.)	1878	1943
DEAKINS, William		1835	1904
, Lydia		1838	1895
DEAN, Joyce			1929
DEARINGER, W. M.		9-15-1823	3- 4-1903
, Martha		1856	1936
, Smith		5- 4-1893	9-21-1897
, Lucy		6-20-1891	9- 2-1896
, Amanda		5-19-1882	11-19-1887
, Infant	son of W. S. M.	8-20-1888	8-20-1888
, Elmer		4-23-1894	
, Mabel G.	(same marker as Elmer D.)	11- 4-1904	No date
, Rosa Doris	d. of Elmer and Mabel D.	8-25-1927	10-25-1933
, Lige T.		1885	1975
DEERING, William J.		1886	1968
, Mary S.		1897	1966
DEES, Charlie H.		1896	1966
, Hallie R.	(same marker as Charlie H. D.)	1896	1972
DELANEY, Joseph A.		1875	1927
, Emma A.	(same marker as Joseph A. D.)	1876	1959
DEMAREE, Jacob		6-14-1819	3-13-1891
, Mary	w. of Jacob D.	12-13-1820	7-13-1908
, Samuel	aged 66yrs 3mos 15das Elder in the old school Presbyterian Church 30yrs.		4-25-1858
, Rachel	Consort of Samuel D. aged 62yrs 11mos 17das		8-11-1857
, Joseph C. S.			9-10-1858
, Lydia			1870
, J. C.	"Surveyor"	9- 9-1859	10-11-1929
, Charles Milton		1868	1923
, Samuel P.		1865	1930
, Lizzie G.	w. of Sam'l P. D.	1871	1897
, G. C. Demaree		1875	1943
, Martha E.	w. of Elder J. M. Demaree	2-28-1839	5-19-1919
, Elder J. M.		8-17-1829	9- 9-1915
, Aunt Bettie		1- 5-1818	5-13-1905
, John O.	"Father" (family marker)	1862	1957
, Ella J.	"Mother" (same marker as John O. D.)	1882	1932
, Samuel H.	Ky. WWII PFC 105 INF 27	7-15-1919	7-10-1944
, Docia V.	(same marker as Sam'l D. & John D.) (On John Demaree family marker)	1908	No date
, Norman Akers	Jean Demaree his wife		No dates
, David Demaree	Ora French his wife		No dates
DENNY, Mary Denny O'Brien		7-19-1856	10-13-1941
, Biddie		1864	1933
DENTON, Laura Katherine		1900	1958

Name	Notes	Born	Died
DICKERSON, H. E.		1861	1920
DITTO, John K.		1875	1940
, Blanche S.		1877	1961
, George Shipman		1904	1973
, Idamae Smith			No date
DONAVAN, Jerry T.		1859	1938
DOUTHITT, A.		1870	1940
, Eve		1870	1948
, Bert T.		1882	1921
, Leonard M.	"Father"	1890	1968
, America V.	"Mother"	1897	No date
DOWDALL, Casandra		5-14-1813	10- 7-1880
DOWDEN, Jimmie Crutchfield		11-10-1895	3-21-1970
, Alice Engels	(same marker as J. C. D.)	9-10-1897	No date
, William E.	"Father"	1878	1961
, Daisy B.	"Mother" (same marker as W. E. D.)	1882	1943
, John C.		1884	1959
DOWNEY, Sol		1881	1963
, Edna		1896	No date
, Eliza Jane		1877	1954
, Noble P.		2-16-1891	3-11-1968
, M. Sue	(same marker as Noble P. D.)	1891	No date
, Tom		1884	1956
, Bertha	(same marker as Tom D.)	1896	19__
, Teresa Ann		1948	1952
DOYLE, M. Dudley		1860	1933
, Cora E.	(same marker as M. Dudley D.)	1877	1943
DUDLEY, C. F.		1845	1925
, Ella		1849	1923
, Clifton R.	s. of C. F. and E. D.	1886	1967
, Sarah E.	d. of C. F. and E. D.	1874	1940
, Lewis M.	s. of C. F. and E. D.	1879	1884
, Ambrose		1862	1938
, Martha		1868	1959
DUNAVAN, Elisha	"Father"	5- 5-1861	9- 9-1917
, Edna	"Mother" (same marker as Elisha)	2- 9-1862	5- 4-1937
, Emil		1869	No date
Lula	(same marker as Emil D.)	1874	1923
, Forest	PFC U.S. ARMY	1-15-1897	6-30-1975
, Irene	(same marker as Forest D.)	1907	No date
, Addie Baugh		1879	12- 1-1923
DUNAVAN-HUDSON (family marker)			
, Nannie T.	"Mother"	1885	1945
, W. P.	"Father"	1885	1944
, George A.	"Daddy"	1901	1967
, Debbie H.		1906	1963
DUNAVAN, James T.	(On Wood family marker)	3- 2-1922	7-16-1949
, Robert A.	aged 22yrs.		10-22-1912
, Rosalie	(w. of Robert A. D.)		No date
, Willie D.		5-26-1888	11-23-1913
, Mattie	(same marker as Willie D.)	11- 1-1888	3- 8-1968
DUNAVANT, A. T.		10-16-1860	No date
, Alice	w. of A. T. D. (same marker)	1-22-1859	9-12-1900
DURBIN, Ruth Davis		1914	1948
EARLEY, James		1891	1916
, Joe D.		1889	1925
, Dora		1869	1948
, Bernice		1893	1929
, Lillian		1895	1926
EASLEY, Frank		1857	1936
, Clemmie	(same marker as Frank E.)	1872	1947
, Samuel W.		1859	1934
, Ella H.		1866	1948
, Virgil S.		1892	1971
, Elzy W.		9-20-1827	6-12-1905
, Catherine	w. of Elzy E.	1834	1917
EASTES, P. A.	"Father"	1858	1935
, Willie Guthrie	"Mother" w. of P. A. E. (same marker)	12-12-1858	8-28-1906
EASTES-HALL-MOORE (family marker)			
, Carrie W.	w. of Guthrie E.	7-26-1882	6-22-1905
EASTES, George T.		1855	1924

Name	Remarks	Born	Died
, Emma	w. of George T. E. (same marker)	1857	1933
, Elmer Boyce	"Father"	1878	1940
, Pearl Nichols	"Mother" (same marker)	1886	1968
, Flossie Harlow		1914	1933
EATON, Phyllis		1906	1973
, Jessie L.	(same marker as Phyllis E.)	1910	No date
EBERSBAKER, G.		11-18-1836	2-19-1925
, Mary Elizabeth	(same marker as G. E.)	8-28-1849	11-28-1921
, G. F.		6-22-1833	1- 2-1910
, Elizabeth	w. of G. F. E.	1-14-1831	1-26-1915
, Albert		8-17-1861	5- 3-1901
, Maggie	w. of A. E.	4-29-1860	12- 5-1895
, Gotthile		12-31-1875	7-20-1903
, William		9-12-1866	2- 1-1955
, Katie	w. of Wm. E.	7-11-1873	9-21-1909
, Liddie		1880	1920
, John W.		1872	1903
, Mollie	(same marker as John W. E.)	1871	1945
, Harry C.		1899	1967
, Fannie Mae	(same marker as Harry C. E.)	1902	No date
, Thomas W.		1874	1954
, Maye Shaw	(same marker as Thomas W. E.)	1894	No date
EBLEN, John Lawson		1844	1929
, Mary Neville	(same marker as John L. E.)	1849	1931
, Hallie		1875	1968
EDDINS, Marvin		2-22-1893	3-20-1944
, Clara		11-10-1895	6-12-1945
, Austin T.		4-28-1860	6-10-1945
, Paul B.		1-18-1907	3-15-1976
EDWARDS, Susan B.	"Mother"		No date
, A. Mitchell	(same marker as Susan B. E.)	1864	1939
, Callie R.	(same marker as A. Mitchell E.)	1867	1955
ELLIS, W. R.		4-12-1828	8-13-1886
, Eliza J.		1832	1916
, James W.		4-11-1860	2-12-1894
, Pryor		4-14-1882	3-13-1931
, Lillie B.	(same marker as Pryor E.)	9-18-1884	12- 5-1975
, Allene Hower	w. of John Morrison E.	11-30-1890	11- 6-1970
, Martha Catherine	d. of J. M. and A. H. E. (infant)		5- 1-1916
, Jesse		1890	1977
, Mattie Todd	(same marker as Jesse E.)	1889	1969
, Petril J.		1916	1917
, Everett C.		2-18-1891	No date
, Jessie M.		4-11-1891	2- 8-1972
, Floyd H.		1895	1968
, Alma W.	(same marker as Floyd H. E.)	1898	1969
, Sallie		4-10-1896	9- 9-1952
, Frank H.	WWII	4- 2-1914	10- 1-1955
, Jessie		6-16-1887	6-16-1959
EMERSON, Hollis		12- 5-1915	3- 4-1935
ERICKSON, Ada		1893	1962
ERWIN, William H.		1871	1938
, Mildred M.		1872	1935
ESTES, Jack		1862	1931
, Sallie A.	w. of Jack E. (same marker)	1865	1952
, John		4- 3-1885	5-18-1959
, William	"Father"	1891	1971
, Cordia A.	"Mother" (same marker as Wm. E.)	1886	1956
, Joel		1912	1921
ETHINGTON, Robert		1842	1916
, Jennie P.		1862	1937
, Virgie	d. of R. and J. E.	10-27-1891	1- 2-1896
, John	(a family marker)	3-12-1837	5-27-1923
, Viana	w. of John E. (same marker)	1-29-1850	3-12-1915
, Charlie	(same marker)	7-19-1875	6-26-1898
, Stella	(same marker)	6-24-1878	No date
, Victor	(same marker)	8- 3-1879	No date
, Nellie	(same marker)	6- 7-1881	2-28-1906
, Lulu	(same marker)	12-14-1882	No date
, James	(same marker)	4-27-1885	No date
, Annie	(same marker)	7- 1-1887	No date

Name	Remarks	Born	Died
, Mayme	(same marker)	3- 8-1891	No date
, Ruth	(same marker)	2- 3-1844	No date
, Willie K. Smith	(same marker)	6- 7-1913	1-23-1925
, Calvert Smith	(same marker)	12- 5-1876	10- 5-1970
, J. Louis		9- 6-1847	1-14-1915
, Kittie	"Mother"	5-13-1858	12-14-1919
, Kitty Jane		1879	1904
, Luther W.	s. of L. W. and Ethel E.	12-21-1903	7-20-1904
, Gracie	d. of J. L. and K. J. E.	8-17-1897	7-29-1898
, Estella	d of J. L. and C. E.	12-20-1892	7- 4-1893
, Tommie	s. of J. L. and C. E.	4-22-1877	3-28-1893
, Thomas Poage		6-29-1853	2-12-1941
, Letitia	w. of Thomas P. E. (same marker)	10- 4-1857	10- 7-1901
, James V.	(same marker)	11- 2-1881	
, Iva	(same marker)	3- 4-1883	No date
, Auburn R.	(same marker)	4- 9-1884	No date
, Claude M.	(same marker)	8-29-1885	1-29-1940
, Lillian S.	(same marker)	10- 6-1887	2- 4-1923
, J. W.		1881	1972
, Nora		1876	1927
, Luther W.		1886	1953
, Ethel Wood	(same marker as Luther E.)	1884	1956
, Victor		1879	1948
, Zilpha		1881	1963
, James		4-27-1885	11-14-1967
, Laura		1- 5-1885	9- 8-1961
, Callie		1882	1906
, L. R.		1894	1942
, Baby		10-17-1914	11-22-1914
, James	(a family marker)	2-13-1798	5-22-1865
, Elenor	w. of James (same marker as Jas.) aged	43yrs.	9- 9-1846
, Eliza J.	(same marker as Jas. E.)	10-12-1823	7-13-1854
, William	(same marker as Jas. E.)	1-16-1825	6-16-1847
, Mary Ann	(same marker as Jas. E.)	6- 6-1827	2- -1859
, Aaron	(same marker as Jas. E.)	3-10-1829	11- 1-1893
, James S.	(same marker as Jas. E.)	4-18-1832	9-23-1856
, Sallie	(same marker as Jas. E.)	3-19-1835	3-25-1902
, John	(same marker as Jas. E.)	3-12-1837	No date
, Martha E.	(same marker as Jas. E.)	2-25-1839	No date
, Robert	(same marker as Jas. E.)	5- 1-1842	No date
, Annie Eliza	w. of James (same marker)	5-12-1821	3-24-1895
, Amanda C.	(same marker as Jas. E.)	10-27-1850	No date
, Thomas P.	(same marker as Jas. E.)	6-29-1853	No date
, Annie Eliza	(same marker as Jas. E.)	3-24-1855	No date
EVANS, William	"Father" (a family marker)	1838	1908
, Malitta	"Mother" (same marker as Wm. E.)	1846	1909
, Harry	(same marker as Wm. E.)	1884	19__
, Mattie E.	(same marker as Wm. E.)	1890	1958
, Harry J.	(same marker as Wm. E.)	1912	1912
EWING, Orve		1876	1955
, Nell S.		1883	No date
, Robert		1888	1969
, Katie Baugh	(same marker as Robert E.)	1888	1967
FALLIS, Herbert T.		1867	1955
, Annie E.	(same marker as Herbert T. F.)	1869	1955
, F. V. (Buck)		7- 9-1899	No date
, Alma K.		7-31-1911	11-19-1963
FARRELL, Walter D.		1865	1932
, Margaret	(same marker as Walter D. F.)	1889	1964
FIGG, Orrend T.	s. of B. J. & I. L.	12-31-189_	5-24-1899
FINK, Walter L.		1894	1973
, Donald W.		1941	1971
FISHBACK, John	"Father"	4- 9-1853	4-10-1923
, Cordelia Frances	w. of John H. F.	4-16-1853	5- 9-1889
, Mary E.	w. of John H. F.	1-29-1862	6-25-1902
, Louis M.		1-16-1883	12-30-1911
, Rushia Harp		8-23-1912	8- 4-1968
FLEXNER, Emile Frank		1895	1972
FLOOD, George W.	"Father"	10-10-1820	1-26-1900
, Margaret	"Mother" w. of George W. F. (same marker)	3-11-1826	11-22-1897

, Monroe		3-25-1825	10-12-1911
, Susan K.	w. of Monroe (same marker)	3-11-1841	12-26-1906
, Mary E.	w. of J. B. Smith and d. of Monroe and Sue Flood	1-28-1866	10-11-1895
, Robert P.	"Husband"	11- 5-1869	10-14-1961
, Mary B. Underwood	"Wife" (same marker)	6- 2-1877	3- 3-1943
, John M.		1861	1938
, Sadie C.	(same marker as John M. F.)	1866	1939
, Robert L.		1902	No date
, Lottie C.	(same marker as Robert L. F.)	1899	No date
, Ruth Flood Calvert		1903	1933
, Charles H.		1840	1931
, Paulina	w. of Chas. H. F. (same marker)	1846	1923
FLOYD-TURNER (family marker)			
, Elijah		1863	1936
, Ella B.	(same marker as Elijah)	1879	1904
, Celestine	(same marker as Elijah) (infant)	1900	1901
, Edward Mason Turner	(same marker)	1873	1957
, Nancy Elizabeth	(same marker)	1896	1974
, Nancy Edwina	(same marker) (infant)		1932
FLOYD, Roy E.	KY PVT HQ CO 20 MW ARMD DIV	2- 8-1911	9-11-1966
FLYNN, J. V. "Bill"		7-28-1888	9- 4-1966
, Ethel		12- 8-1896	8- 5-1938
, James Samuel		5-14-1921	1- 6-1925
, Earnest		9- 2-1891	1-23-1928
, Rosa	(same marker as Earnest)	9-11-1904	No date
, Gayle L.		No date	2-15-1925
FORD, Mary		7-29-1772	5-23-1854
FORTNER, Chester R.		1884	1933
, Leonia		1883	1917
FORQUER, Ruth Heaton McCarty (FAUQUIER)		1887	1954
FRANCK, Val F.		No date	2-18-1868
, Sara B.		No date	12-18-1948
FRAZIER, Frank	aged 79yrs.		3-12-1940
, Ernest		1891	1944
, John Wesley	"Father"	5-27-1882	11-11-1952
, Flora Bishop	"Mother"	2- 6-1883	3- 3-1959
, John Russell	KY PVT HQ CO 20 BW ARMD DIV	2- 8-1911	9-11-1966
, Leonis	PVT WWI USA	2-17-1887	10-23-1975
FROST, Emmett		1871	1964
, Maggie	(same marker as Emmett)	1872	1953
, Emmett N.		1904	1950
, Norma P.		1893	1956
, Herman E.		1899	No date
, Sarah K.	(same marker as Herman)	1901	1973
, William V.		1-25-1901	11-29-1974
FURNISH, Thomas L.		3-11-1884	9-22-1974
, Bertha M.		4-24-1887	12-10-1952
GARDNER, Chester R.		1884	1963
, Jess Lee		1885	1966
, Mamie A.		1887	No date
GARNER, Nannie		5-31-1845	8- 3-1878
GARRETT, Edward A.		1843	1911
, James A.		1841	1914
, Jessie E.		4-23-1876	4- 9-1885
GARVEY, Samuel T.		1849	1901
, Elizabeth		1852	1918
, Leota E.		1880	1906
GERMAN, Elizabeth		1873	1939
GIBSON, John T.		2- 9-1823	7-23-1891
, William S.		2-15-1835	1-14-1916
, Francis	(same marker as Wm. S. G.)	5- 2-1843	5-29-1932
, Minnie	w. of W. S. Gibson and d. of W. B. and R. L. Neal	2-15-1838	12-25-1869
, Lillie		1862	1942
GILBERT, Bessie Clack	w. of Sam'l E. Gilbert	11-10-1886	12-12-1971
, E. Hayden		1877	1957
, Lucy Clark	(same marker as E. Hayden)	1883	1976
GILES, George W.		12-12-1904	10-25-1961
GILL, Mary E.	w. of B. F. Gill	5-26-1860	6-20-1883

Name	Remarks	Born	Died
GILL-HUGHES (family marker)			
, Chester Earl Gill		1879	1942
, Maryline H.	(same marker)	1881	1968
, Buddie	(same marker)	1871	1954
, Lenora	(same marker)	1868	1953
, Buddie Hughes Gill	WWII	3-20-1906	11- 6-1954
GILL, Jerry		1903	1955
, Lillian		1906	19__
GIVIDEN-BIBB (family marker)			
, Joe J. Gividen		12- 3-1880	4- 4-1949
, Beulah M.		8-26-1883	No date
GIVIDEN, Joe		1856	No date
, Sarah M.	w. of Joe Gividen (same marker)	1856	1923
, William H.		5-31-1883	1-17-1957
, Mary E. Shannon		7-27-1889	10-14-1961
, Nellie E.	d. of Joe and S. M. G.	8-12-1897	9- 1-1897
, Phynus	s. of Joe and S. M. G.	4-16-1885	3-15-1899
, John A.		12-10-1878	7- 3-1902
, Earl		8-29-1901	3-27-1902
GLENN, Lena H.		1886	1973
GODFREY, J. C.		12- 2-1861	3-24-1937
, Elizabeth	(same marker as J. C. G.)	8-24-1865	10-19-1948
, John C.	Spanish American War		No date
GOLDEN, Elmo Guy		5- 5-1894	10-27-1963
, Rena Belle		4- 3-1895	6-25-1973
, Charles B.		9- 2-1868	11-15-1957
, Minnie A.		6-30-1870	5-23-1950
, Elza C.		1915	No date
, Dorothy A.	(same marker as Elza G.)	1920	No date
GOODRICH, Wallace C.		1900	1924
GOODWIN, Dr. O. P.		1875	1954
, Lola C.	(same marker as Dr. O. P. G.)	1883	1963
, James S.		1907	1923
GORDON, Mary E.	w. of J. M. Gordon	1812	1904
, R. Watt	"Father"	1846	1935
, Nannie S.	"Mother" (same stone as R. Watt G.)	1856	1945
, Richard W.		1887	1958
, Virginia R.		1893	1955
, George		1885	1887
, Mary Emma		1888	1890
, Garnett		1891	1892
, Lizzie Mae	infant		No date
, Willie		1896	1904
, Arch		9-10-1855	9- 9-1950
, Arthur		1-22-1880	3- 5-1968
, Roud		11-28-1885	No date
, Anna	(same marker as Roud G.)	11- 7-1888	12-15-1960
, William H.		1871	1963
, Artie J.	(same marker as Wm. H. G.)	1862	1965
, Luther		1882	No date
, Mildred	(same marker as Luther G.)	1386	1962
, Make		1880	1964
, Julia		1882	1964
, Beckham		1903	1967
, Linnie		1918	No date
, Orville		9- 2-1890	9-24-1969
, Ida B. Rodgers	(same marker as Orville)	1896	1976
, Howard		2-10-1890	9-20-1968
, Lizzie Ellis	(same marker as Howard)	2-17-1891	12- 3-1974
, Virgil		1894	1973
, Myrtle E.	(same marker as Virgil)	1895	1972
, Horace		12-18-1914	No date
, Nellie B.		12- 2-1917	1-20-1931
GRAVES, (first name not given)		1896	1941
, James T.	"Father"	1870	1947
, Mary E.	"Mother" w. of Jas. T. G. (same marker)	1886	1911
, Mary E.		1906	1918
, Charles M.		5-20-1908	3-21-1966
, James P.	MM3 USN WWII	8- 2-1910	6-28-1975
, Arthur		1885	1920
, Mildred		1916	1920

GREEN, John F.	(same marker as Lucy)	3- 3-1836	No date
, Lucy G.	w. of John F. Sr.	12-29-1842	11-25-1903
, Robert Walton	s. of T. A. and L. M. G.	11-16-1886	8-17-1887
GREENE, Bedford		1894	1920
, Sallie		1871	1936
, Nelson		1870	1955
GREENWELL, J. L. family marker		1842	1927
, Mary A.	(same marker as J. L. G.)	1854	1940
, Charles	(same marker as J. L. G.)	1888	1912
, Effie L.	(same marker as J. L. G.)	1886	1948
GRIBSY, William P.		6-14-1874	8- 8-1957
, Rosa Etta	(same marker as Wm. P. G.)	2- 6-1873	6-17-1944
GRIMES, Jennie W.	"Daughter"	1888	1969
GRUGAN, Joshua		1865	1944
, Lucinda S.	(same marker as Joshua G.)	1873	1959
GUTHRIE, William		1818	1877
, Elizabeth A.	(same marker as Wm. G.)	1822	1895
, J. T.		1860	1946
, Virginia J.	(same marker as J. T. G.)	1862	1943
HACKETT, Minnie Wallace		12- 5-1876	7- 6-1966
, Hiram		1887	1937
, Mildred		1890	1962
, Curtis		1907	1933
HALE, Arthur Pearl		1911	No date
, Omar		1906	1966
HALL, Elizabeth	wife of J. J. Hall	2-26-1790	8-14-1850
, John I.		7-22-1792	7- 9-1880
, Elizabeth	wife of John I. Hall	11- -1790	8-14-1850
, Alley	wife of John I. Hall	12-27-1793	8-26-1878
, W. S.		11-20-1817	5-21-1887
, Arthur	s. of D. P. and Lula Hall	7-15-1886	10-24-1886
, Dudley	"Father"	2-26-1824	3- 3-1889
, M. E.	w. of Dudley H. "Mother"	9- 5-1830	4-20-1907
, Infant	d. of (illegible)		1884
, Shelby	s. of (illegible)	1878	1879
, Squire		12-25-1823	10-22-1906
, Lucy	w. of Squire Hall	1826	1890
, Wesley		1848	1942
, Lucy Ellen		1865	1935
, Georgie	d. of S. and L. H.	2-24-1862	10-15-1881
, Nancy	w. of Thos. J. Hall	1- 8-1825	5-21-1879
, T. J.		1850	1928
, Mollie B.		1861	1947
, A. W.		10-10-1844	11- 5-1884
, Melissa E.		3-11-1840	2-18-1909
, Otto	s. of A. W. and M. E.	9- 4-1884	9- 4-1884
HALL-BUFORD, Charles A. (a family marker)		1832	1897
, Sarah Ann Rankin	w. of Charles A. H. (s.m.)	1839	1914
HALL, Martha Hieatt		1833	1915
, William B.		1844	1917
, Everett		1862	1936
, Mary	w. of W. M.	1- 9-1818	3-19-1890
, Mattie	d. of J. W. and L. Hall	12-11-1890	1- 8-1891
, Albert T.		9- 2-1850	9- 4-1890
, John G.		1854	1914
, Annie J.	(same marker as John G. H.)	1863	1937
HALL-ESTES-MOORE (a family marker)			
, Sam		1-11-1843	4-22-1921
, M. A.	(same marker as Sam Hall)	12-16-1859	No date
HALL, Lemuel B.		1857	1914
, Bettie		1858	1882
, Mollie E.		1861	1895
, Annie S.		1871	1955
, Birdie	d. of L. B. and M. E. H.	2-28-1884	9- 8-1884
, Henry C.		1-24-1858	5- 5-1937
, Mary B.		8-22-1870	4-10-1962
, Jamieson B.		3-12-1888	10-30-1923
, Arthur C.		1- 8-1891	8-12-1894
, Lydia	w. of Joe Hall	1866	1940
, Benjamin T.		1865	1948

Name	Note	Born	Died
, Ira		1865	1930
, Laura Reese	w. of Tra Hall	1869	1953
, Parthenia	w. of John Hall	7-17-1852	12-15-1900
, Clarence		9- 2-1874	12-28-1927
, Mattie	(same marker as Clarence H.)	12-12-1873	12-28-1927
, Jim	"Brother"	1-13-1885	10- 8-1920
, Gracy	d. of Omer and Ona Hall	6-17-1901	5- 8-1902
, Clarence Nolan		8-31-1874	2-19-1928
, Vivian Kesler		4- 6-1881	1-15-1968
, Allen		1909	1913
, Willie D.		10- 7-1879	10-20-1904
, Amanda R.	(same marker as Willie D.)	8-15-1878	No date
, Kittie		4- 8-1879	2-18-1947
, Orlester	KY PVT 338 INF	2- 4-1887	1-22-1957
, Eugene	KY MECH 11 COAST ARTY	No date	11- 1-1942
, John W.	KY PVT D9 BN 3 DIV	2-21-1889	3-13-1964
, Della M.	(same marker as John)	1900	No date
, Omega M.	(same marker as John & Della)	1926	No date
, John Homer		1898	No date
, Daisy Dean	(same marker as John Homer)	1899	1977
, J. Kenneth	(same marker as John H. & Daisy)	1919	No date
, Nora Frances	(same marker as J. Kenneth)	1917	1976
, Hilton P.		1887	1955
, Mary B.	w. of Hilton P.	1890	1913
, Isaiah G.		1887	1943
, Pearl		2-18-1889	3-30-1959
, James A.		11-20-1906	7- 8-1959
, Johnnie	"Husband"	1887	1950
, Helen T.	"Wife" (same marker as Johnnie)	1894	1973
, Alonzo	"Husband" (same marker as Johnnie)	1880	1938
, Dora B.	"Wife" (same marker as Alonzo)	1879	1937
, Kessler R.		11-28-1900	1-16-1970
, Alpha Davis	(same marker as Kessler)	10-29-1900	No date
, Albert R.	CPL USA WWII	7-17-1913	4- 1-1975
, James B.		1881	1973
, Callie	(same marker as James B.)	1880	1971
, Kenneth E.	MSGT USA WWII	11-26-1907	12-21-1977
, Christine	(same marker as Kenneth E.)	1911	No date
, Albert H.		1884	1957
, Lydia M.		1891	1957
, Lester G.	KY TEC 5 1st ARMD DV WWII	12-24-1916	4-30-1943
HAMILTON, L. P.		1890	1941
HAMMOND, Goodlow W.		9-29-1859	2-18-1898
, Sallie Hammond Riner		8-29-1870	3-10-1949
, Raymond	s. of Goodlow	1-13-1890	2-26-1891
, Jennie Shipman		1890	1940
, Harold K.		1891	No date
, L. T.		1884	1960
, Allie Banta		1878	1968
, Johnston Lee		1893	1918
, Elizabeth Shuck	(same marker as Johnston Lee)		No dates
HANCE, Clemie		1893	No date
, Hessie	(same marker as Clemie)	1897	No date
, Gale Lee		1939	1943
, Joseph R.		1- 9-1943	1-14-1943
, Ramona J.		1962	1962
HANCOCK, T. H.		1844	1925
, Ellen Banta	(same marker as T. H.)	1854	1914
, O. B.		1873	1928
HANKINS, Robert Emmett		1878	1955
, Lucy Collett		1870	1949
, Willis Glenn		7- 9-1941	1-10-1960
, Avis Joan		1-27-1940	No date
HARDESTY, James W.	"Father"	2-13-1857	11-10-1910
, Sue M.	"Mother" (same marker as James)	9- 9-1864	11-24-1958
, Greta Celeste	d. of J. W. and S. M. H.	1894	1896
, Leonard C.		5-27-1888	10-24-1939
, Ben F.		1871	1952
, Mary L.		1878	1966
, Roy Hunter		2-25-1901	7-22-1901
HARDIN, W. E.		1868	1923

Name	Note	Born	Died
, Cora		1876	1923
, James J.	"Father"	1872	1955
, Lena Batts	"Mother"	1876	1934
, Tom		1878	1965
, Ella Purvis	(same marker as Tom)	1884	1958
HARDING, Capt. John	"Soldier of the Revolution"		No date
In memory of			
, Thomas	"Soldier of the Revolution"	1758	1842
, Aaron	(same marker as John and Thomas)	1805	1874
, Sarah Moss	"and their wives" (same marker)		No date
, Sarah Payne	"and their wives" (same marker)		No date
, Margaret Campbell	"and their wives" (same marker)		No date
, Jack	(same marker as above)	4- 1-1843	7-24-1915
, Susie Downs	(same marker as above)	5-16-1851	9- 9-1939
, Jack	(same marker as above)	9-16-1881	12-10-1912
HARFORD, Mahalie	(same marker as R. H.)	11-21-1844	8- 2-1925
, R. H.	(same marker as Mahalie & Henr.)	8-14-1847	1- 4-1920
, Henrietta	(same marker as R. H. & M.)	8-12-1849	11-11-1884
HARLOW, Nancy		1847	1919
, George W.		1850	1941
, Jemina	(same marker as George W.)	1860	1939
, George W.		1866	1931
, Mickey H.	(same marker as George W.)	1877	19__
, Richard Eli		1890	1942
, Lola Bishop	(same marker as Richard Eli)	1897	1970
, John W.		3-31-1860	12- 3-1951
, Mary Barton	(same marker as John W.)	1-16-1868	6-15-1941
, Horace		12- 8-1894	8-23-1971
, Annie F.	(same marker as Horace)	9-25-1896	No date
, Earl W.		1900	1943
, Alfred	"Daddy"	10-24-1911	7- 4-1977
HARNER, W. P.		5- 7-1872	2-25-1902
HARP, Mordica		1881	1960
, Katherine L.	(same marker as Mordica)	1890	1971
, Grover C.		1885	1968
, Jennie S.		1880	1930
, Bunk		1890	1935
, Lucy C.	(same marker as Bunk)		No dates
, Lizzie Wilhite	"Mother"	9- 6-1908	11-11-1945
, James M.		9-25-1917	6-20-1966
HARPER, Silas D.		1876	1950
, Maggie C.	(same marker as Silas D.)	1877	1959
, Bill		1883	1953
, Flora	(same marker as Bill)	1887	1970
HARTFORD, Squire E.	"Father"	12-16-1855	9-24-1919
, Mary A. McAlister	"Mother" w. of and same marker as Squire E.	3-21-1863	4-23-1919
HARTMAN, Frank		1816	1885
, Melanie Raisor	w. of and same marker as Frank		No dates
, C. C.		1863	1944
, Susan M.	(same marker as C. C.)	1861	1936
, Henry	World War I	11-17-1887	2- 3-1974
, Orlester	World War I	8- 9-1895	5-22-1970
, Katie Noe		1902	1940
, John		2-17-1849	No date
, Jessie A. Galbreth	w. of and same marker as John	9-15-1846	10- 5-1905
HARTMAN-SHANNON family marker			
, Frank		1878	1956
, Linnie P.	(same marker)	1886	No date
, Chester	(same marker)	1880	1951
, Hattie M.	(same marker)	1884	1967
HATCHELL, William		1871	1946
HAWKINS-JOHNSTON family marker			
, W. H. Hawkins		1873	1974
, Maggie	w. of William Hawkins	10-29-1886	1- 3-1908
HEAD, John H.		1853	1922
, Enos S.	(same marker as John H.)	1887	1916
, Mary Ann		1880	1957
HEATON, Elton		1892	1965
, Bernice C.	(same marker as Elton)	1905	No date
, Lola		1889	1977

Name	Notes	Born	Died
, Mary	(same marker as Lola)	1895	1973
HEIGHTCHEW, W. S.		1852	illegible
, M_____ A.	illegible	1859	1905
HIGHTCHEW , Frank		1890	1920
, Rena Heightchew James		1888	1964
, Maynard		1897	1967
, Ida Reese	(same marker as Maynard)	1901	1975
, Melvin J.		4-21-1917	12-15-1918
, Obie		1892	1957
, Louise N.		1925	1952
, Estile	(same marker as Louise N.)	1921	No date
, Rudolph		1924	1926
HEILMAN, William H.	"Father"	1871	1944
, Lula A.	"Mother"	1884	No date
, Roland T.		1872	1917
, Alice N.	w. of Roland T. (same marker)	1873	1925
, Lorena G.	(same marker as Roland and Alice)	1912	1914
, Lester E.		1906	1956
, Mary Marshall		1913	1963
, Leonard		1878	1958
, Sarah Margaret Mitchell	(same marker as Leonard)	1882	1941
, Clarence Thomas		1909	1920
HELTON, Woodrow			No dates
, Helen	(same marker as Woodrow)		No dates
HEMDERSON, Noble S.	"Father"	1872	1952
, Martha F.	"Mother"	1871	1952
, Bertha		10-24-1886	8- 4-1953
, Guy		4- 1-1893	12- 1-1929
, Genevieve		4-16-1917	9-30-1936
HENDERSON-CASEY family marker			
, James M.		1874	1962
, Dora J.		1869	1944
HENDERSON, Annie P.		1886	1944
, Joseph Harrison		12-27-1892	5-28-1977
, Bessie Slattery	(same marker as J.)	11- 8-1897	No date
, John Thomas		1878	1944
, Addie Buford	(same marker as John Thomas)	1879	1944
, W. Horace	(same marker as John Thomas)	1882	1963
, Ida Belle Buford	(same marker as W. Horace)	1883	1923
, W. Howard		5-21-1904	No date
, Alma Cox	(same marker as W. Howard)	8-24-1911	No date
, Charles Allen	(same marker as W. Howard)	7- 7-1905	8- 5-1966
, Lora Hughes	(same marker as Charles Allen)	10-25-1905	No date
, William F.		1893	1962
, James T.	(same marker as William F.)	1916	1957
, Jeannie J.	(same marker as James T.)	1920	1955
, Randel Dale		No date	5- 8-1952
HENSLEY, Daniel		1873	1957
, Rosie Sparks	(same marker as Daniel)	1877	1957
, Silas	(same marker as Daniel)	1378	1959
, Linda J.		10-21-1940	8-17-1967
HERRELL, Ernest R.		1890	1967
, Frankie M.	(same marker as Ernest R.)	1890	1976
, Sherfy		1896	1966
, Nellie E.	(same marker as Sherfy)	1897	No date
HILL, George M.		6-21-1839	9- 2-1879
, Amanda L.		11-13-1839	5-16-1881
, Henry Scott	s. of Geo. M. & A. H.	11- 4-1867	7- 9-1868
, Fletcher S.		8-20-1870	1-25-1893
, Margaret Belwood	w. of Rev. F. M. Hill	1885	1908
HINKEY, John		1848	1919
HOCKENSMITH, Llewellyn E.		1887	1958
, Bessie Cawby		1894	1973
HOLLAND, J. W.		9- 2-1848	2-15-1908
, Sarah F.	w. of J. W. (same marker)	8-24-1845	6-28-1906
, Will		5-14-1871	9-22-1911
, Reuben C.		1873	1946
, Florence P.		1875	1948
, Ernest	World War I	2-21-1887	11-10-1961
HOLLAND-KING family marker			

Name	Note	Born	Died
, Joseph M.		1876	1946
, Pearl M.		1877	1969
HOLLEY, Thomas		4- 1-1830	1-10-1883
, A. J. H.	"Mother'	No date	No date
, W. H. H.		No date	No date
HOLLOWAY, Lorenzo D.		1-21-1823	11- 5-1916
, Elizabeth		11-15-1818	12-23-1818
, Emily V.		9- 1-1844	4-25-1907
HORTON, Nell M.		1890	1951
HOWER, Thomas J.		1862	1921
, Amanda S.		1865	1924
, Patterson		1890	1951
, Forest Ray	s. of T. J. & A. M.	5-29-1893	11-13-1896
, Peter		7-16-1829	12-14-1908
, Martha J.	w. of Peter	7-28-1844	3- 7-1913
, Corda E.		2- 2-1889	4- 1-1890
, Peter Jr.		1-14-1867	4- 9-1945
, Martha Smith		9-17-1869	1- 7-1950
HUDSON-DUNAVAN family marker			
, W.P.	"Father"	1885	1944
, Nannie T.	"Mother"	1885	1945
HUDSON, J. R.		1856	1918
Annie E.		1862	1946
, Infant	son of J. R. & A. E. H.	1-27-1883	8- 5-1884
, Lillie R.	d. of J. R. & A. E. H.	9-26-1881	11-29-1881
, Harry W.		1870	1957
, Lena R.	(same marker as Harry W.)	1872	1966
, Albert V.	s. of H. W. & L. P. H.	3-14-1902	7-30-1902
, Goebel B.		10-26-1899	12-24-1976
HUGHES, John W.		8-15-1825	3-20-1896
, Marharet		10-29-1844	No date
, Lenora		4-22-1874	1- 5-1886
, Arthur Ricketts		1878	1953
, Kate Maddox		1880	1960
, Michael		4-16-1862	1- 1-1949
, Cordelia	(same marker as Michael)	7-13-1866	11-13-1903
, Ambrose	"Father"	1866	1934
, Ollie	"Mother" (same marker as Ambrose)	1874	1919
HUMSTON-SCOBEE family marker			
, Lester		1887	1913
HUNDLEY, James S.		1875	No date
, Louella R.	(same marker as James S.)	1875	1950
, Baker		1881	1963
, Lenna K.		1883	1974
, Gayle		1883	1931
IRELAND, Jennie		1858	1939
, Richmond	PVT 3RD KY INFANTRY	No date	11- 3-1942
, Thomas C.		1823	1906
, Margaret		1836	1901
, Joseph W.		1877	1907
IVERS, J. H.		8-17-1831	4- 1-1899
, Thomas F.		1865	1951
, Nancy Harp	(same marker as Thomas F.)	1879	1952
, Donald J.		1933	1958
, E. J.	"Father"	1833	1911
, Elizabeth	"Mother" (same marker as E. J.)	1849	No date
, Oscar		1866	1953
, Bettie		1863	1941
JACKSON, Elizabeth E.	w. of Rev. Andrew Jackson	12-30-1845	5-29-1915
, Elijah W.	"Father"	1887	1971
, Blanche T.	"Mother" (same marker as Elijah W.)	1893	1971
, Emma L.	"Daughter" (same marker as E. W. & B. T.)	1917	No date
, Theodore L.		10-19-1891	7-27-1975
, Roberta S.	(same marker as Theodore)	10-21-1893	7-30-1974
, Robert C.	World War II	6-27-1919	4- 5-1967
JACOBY, William		3-30-1810	3-27-1888
, Mary	w. of William J.	1816	1-21-1897
, James M.	s. of William & Mary J.	4-21-1840	4-25-1862
, William H.		7-21-1845	2-21-1885
, Isaac Newton		9- 2-1849	1-26-1932
, Carrie S.		1- 3-1855	3-11-1928

, "Little Newt."	s. of I. N. & C. S. Jacoby	2-14-1885	2-21-1892
, Lorenzo M.		1-18-1883	12-21-1968
, John P.		1-30-1835	7- 4-1890
, Melissa D.	w. of John P. Jacoby	12-23-1843	10- 9-1910
, Mary A.		4-19-1862	3-27-1882
, Fred H.	"Husband"	5-10-1895	2-19-1944
, Isaac N.		1846	1936
, Martha J. Hill		1850	1894
, James Egbert		1865	1923
, Henry Oscar		12-17-1869	3- 6-1904
, Josephine		3- 8-1887	12-21-1887
, Raymond		1893	1894
JAMES, David		3-10-1828	6-15-1915
, Lydia	w. of David (same marker)	1-19-1836	No date
, E. T.	"Father"	1836	1922
, Josephine	"Mother" w. of E. T.	1841	1922
, R. W.		11-15-1863	8- 4-1921
, H. B.		1865	1938
, Jennie		1866	1961
, E. Thomas		1868	No date
, Minnie M.	(same marker as E. Thomas)	1878	1952
, Rena Heightchew James		1888	1964
, Rachel F.		1854	1922
, Newton		1887	No date
, Cordia H.	(same marker as Newton)	1889	1956
, Earl C.	"Son"	1918	1922
, W. L.		7-20-1849	10-15-1905
, Sarah A.		1- 4-1855	10-23-1910
, Dillon	"Father"	1858	1942
, Arvenia	w. of Dilen James	4- 2-1872	12- 1-1910
, Laura Clark	"Mother"	1889	1964
, Edmond T. Jr.		5-14-1860	8- 1-1934
, Sarah Alice	(same marker as Edmond)	8-22-1862	9- 4-1924
, Willie		1868	1940
, Emma T.	(same marker as Willie)	1871	1941
, Herbert	World War I	1-13-1895	10-23-1965
, John		1896	1939
, Maggie	(same marker as John)	1908	No date
, Winfred B.		1873	1953
, Gertrude S.	(same marker as Winfred B.)	1872	1941
, Linden		1873	1958
, Susie	(same marker as Linden)	1873	1957
, Fount M.	"Father"	1872	1957
, Annie D.	"Mother" (same marker as Fount)	1874	1936
, Willie F.		1911	No date
, Christine E.		1916	1945
, Herbert J.		1890	1967
, Ada J.	(same marker as Herbert J.)	1893	1974
, Ralph M.	PVT USA World War II	1917	1978
, Charlie	"Husband"	3-16-1892	11-16-1965
, Birdie S.	"Wife" (same marker as Charlie)	4-16-1891	No date
, Hazel		1915	1918
, Ellene F.		1918	1919
, Silas		1890	1965
, Rosalie	(same marker as Silas)	1893	No date
, Chester A.		1897	No date
, Velma W.		1899	1967
, Russell		1900	No date
, Ella O.	(same marker as Russell)	1901	1973
, Ronald Len		No date	1947
Emzy		1883	1954
JENNINGS, Amos		1858	1930
, Agnes		1868	1950
, Samuel T.		1885	1913
, Leonard	KY PFC CO A 116 INF WWII	3-23-1917	5-26-1967
, Linda Bright	(same marker as Leonard)	7-18-1921	No date
, Erving		1890	1939
, Blanche	(same marker as Erving)	1893	1976
, William Russell	s. of E. & B. Jennings	12-10-1912	3- 9-1913
, Celina		10- 6-1914	9-11-1976
JESSEE, Mary Claxon	w. of J. F. Jessee	4- 8-1867	11-13-1896

, John Willis	"Father"	1877	1944
, Daisy E.	"Mother"	1880	1977
, James A.		1877	1961
, Ida M.		1881	1964
, James Allen	S SGT AIR FORCE WWII	7-20-1909	5- 8-1957
JOHNSON, Joe	KY PFC CO A 116 INF WWII	3-23-1917	5-26-1967
JOHNSTON, H. P.		6- 2-1810	6-20-1892
, James J.		8-25-1826	7-25-1902
, Elizabeth K.	(same marker as James J.)	7-30-1829	4- 7-1905
, Robbie R.	(same marker as James J.)	8-11-1866	4- 5-1901
, Charlie Butler	(same marker as J. J.)	8-17-1886	6-16-1906
, Capt. I. N.	6th KY INF CO H	5-11-1833	1-26-1928
, Annie Nash	w. of Capt. I. N. Johnston	10-12-1841	4-24-1914
, In memory of infants of	J. B. & A. E. Johnston		No dates
, Henry S.		12-14-1856	12-24-1906
, Annie E.	w. of Henry S. (same marker)	No date	9- 4-1924
, Otto		4- 6-1888	6-21-1970
, Rose	(same marker as Otto)	8- 6-1886	12-12-1949
, Joseph E.		1875	1970
, Stella W.	(same marker as Joseph E.)	1876	1960
JOHNSTON-HAWKINS family marker			
, R. H.		1865	1934
, Alice		1867	1936
JONES, Warren		1848	1936
, Viane	w. of Warren (same marker)	1855	1922
, George		1876	1955
, Margaret	(same marker as George)	1873	1952
, Leonard J.		1882	1974
, Haidee L.	(same marker as Leonard J.)	1888	1939
, Tom		1890	1947
, Maud Smith		1893	1974
, William "Pete"		1895	1966
, Lorene F.	(same marker as William)	1902	No date
, George W.		2-22-1900	7-19-1974
, Willie Mae		6-26-1901	5- 6-1976
, Willie C.	SGT 779 BASE UNIT AAF KY WWII	1- 4-1909	2-17-1967
, E. D., M.D.		12- 4-1846	1- 9-1917
, Martha H.		4- 1-1845	1-16-1887
, Anna Holliday		11-10-1869	1- 1-1939
, Bernice H.		2-19-1878	10- 5-1896
KAVANAUGH, Joe		10-17-1881	5-23-1960
, Pearl		10-27-1876	12-24-1958
, William B.	PVT 1st BTRY FIELD ARTY KY	8-31-1880	2-27-1962
, Maude C.	(same marker as William B.)	5- 1-1883	11-27-1970
KEENAN, A. J.		1860	1939
, Annie B.	w. of A. J. (same marker)	1870	1923
. Oron		1888	1942
, Lena	(same marker as Oron)	1886	1948
KELLY, James F.		6-27-1800	5-16-1872
, Melissa	w. of James F. Kelly	8-14-1807	3-16-1845
, Lucinda Jane	d. of J. F. & M. Kelly	11-28-1838	4- 2-1851
, Casander	d. of James F. & Melissa Kelly	7- 3-1833	3- 4-1843
, Caleb		1840	1926
, Frances	w. of Caleb (same marker)	1852	1923
, Elmo		9- 1-1916	8-21-1932
, Ola F.		1898	1975
, Maynie	(same marker as Ola F.)	1897	1963
, John F.		1840	1925
, George L.		1883	1953
, Lena R.		1889	1972
, John B.	"Father"	1860	1928
, Mary Hance	"Mother" (same marker as John B.)	1869	1938
, Jea O.		1878	1929
, Lawrence		1889	1951
, Eliza Martin	(same marker as Lawrence)	1894	1956
, Jennie L.		1869	1946
, Leonard	"Father"	1873	1942
, Phoebie	"Mother" (same marker as Leonard)	1870	1932
, Ive		1888	1961
, Orban		1893	1927
, Anna	(same marker as Orban)	1900	No date

Name	Remarks	Born	Died
, Roy		1893	1977
, Mattie H.	(same marker as Roy)	1894	19__
, Roy		1900	1957
KELLEY, Dan		1845	1908
, Anne	(same marker as Dan)	1856	1925
, John Thomas		1851	1899
, Nancy J.		1858	1941
, George W.		1858	1949
, Amanda B.	(same marker as George W.)	1866	1947
, Samuel		1862	1951
, Maggie	"Mother"	1865	1937
, G. Humphrey		1882	1977
, Muriel M.	(same marker as G. Humphrey)	1884	1956
, James M.		1889	1954
, Wava C.	(same marker as James M.)	1889	1976
, Charles		1912	1929
, John I.		1870	1914
, Flora A.		1875	1930
, Anna Kelley Leitz		1904	1930
, Lillard		1870	1943
, Molly	(same marker as Lillard)	1871	1951
, Edd		1875	1957
, Nana	(same marker as Edd)	1881	No date
, John		12- 3-1871	5- 5-1940
, Fanny		9-17-1874	11-23-1936
, Harry R.		8- 3-1905	1- 8-1929
, Pauline		1926	1929
, William		3- 6-1868	2-15-1957
, Laura B.	(same marker as William)	1876	1964
, Daphine	d. of Wm & Laura K. (same marker)	1913	1919
, Fred		1879	1955
, Myrtle	(same marker as Fred)	1882	1938
, Luther		1882	1973
, Ellar	(same marker as Luther)	1884	1963
, Nolalee		11-30-1906	10-19-1911
, Minnis		5- 3-1893	1- 7-1926
, Fannie	"Mother" (same marker as Minnis)	11-11-1865	No date
, James W.		9- 3-1889	12-24-1971
, James Hester		8- 8-1913	11- 4-1918
, Raymon		4-18-1896	No date
, Mary B.		1-18-1896	5-10-1973
, Cantrall	KY PFC USA WWII	9-26-1923	8-26-1973
KEMPER, William T.		3-11-1853	5- 4-1891
, Rebecca A.		1853	1925
, Annie		1872	1946
, Obie		1880	1965
, Belle Peyton	(same marker as Obie)	1892	No date
, Roy C.		1899	1943
, Mary K.	(same marker as Roy C.)	1905	No date
KEPHART, Grandmother Eliza A.		10-10-1814	9- 5-1899
, J. M.		3- 1-1818	12-13-1895
, Elizabeth	w. of J. M. Kephart	2-13-1834	3-26-1901
, Delmar		1909	1919
, James A.		10-30-1847	1- 7-1881
, Mattie		12- 5-1855	5- 4-1885
, Tommie S.		1876	1920
, Jacob W.		1878	1941
, Fannie M.		1885	1962
, Thomas	aged 60years	No date	No date
, J. E.		1857	1926
, J. H.		1864	1927
, Nannie V.	w. of William H. Kephart	3-17-1864	8-11-1881
, Web F.		7-29-1861	11- 9-1933
, Mattie Demaree	w. of Web K. (same marker)	5-26-1866	9-28-1894
, Baby	son of W. F. & M. D. K. (same marker)	No date	No date
, Bettie	"Mother" (same marker)	6-16-1832	9- 6-1901
, Mount J.	"Daddy"	1868	1953
, Jeanett R.	"Mother"	1882	1975
, Mattie Johnston		1876	1934
, Elmer		1890	1949
, Bessie	(same marker as Elmer)	1888	1971

Name	Notes	Born	Died
KESLER, Paul		4-23-1885	1-15-1968
, Carrie Scobee	(same marker as Paul)	1-26-1888	No date
, Isaac N.		1858	1912
, Margaret	w. of Isaac N. S. (same marker)	1862	1958
, John W.	s. of Isaac N. & Margaret K.	1-29-1883	1-27-1907
KEY, Ida Ridgeway		No date	1-10-1907
KINCAID, Blanche N.		1894	1932
KING, Jed M.	(King-Holland family marker)	1902	No date
, Nell Frances		1906	No date
KISTNER, William F.		6-14-1880	10-26-1956
, Georgia H.	(same marker as William)	4-19-1881	12- 1-1953
, Frank J.		8-10-1874	9- 5-1952
, Eva		12-13-1870	1-24-1950
, Edith Quisenberry		1918	1968
KITSON, W. E.	"Father"	4- 8-1823	11-16-1892
, Serelda J.	"Mother" w. of W. E. Kitson	7-16-1825	2- 3-1903
,	"Father" (round stone pillow without name)		No dates
, Eliza S.	"Mother" w. of J. W. Kitson	4-16-1855	4-29-1893
, S. E.		Illegible	189_
, Nannie		12-13-1863	10- 7-1931
, Gardner		1868	1947
, Annie Kemper		1873	1958
, Lennie		1885	1952
, Bertha Mitchell	(same marker as Lennie)	1892	1965
, Linden	KY PVT 31ST US VOL	No date	7- 8-1943
, Emmet B.		1887	1957
, Alpha Bergen	(same marker as Emmet B.)	1887	1973
KNIGHT, Mary	w. of T. Knight	1-21-1821	4- 9-1849
, Frank		4-26-1851	5-13-1919
, Ida B.	w. of Frank Knight	8-24-1865	7-30-1912
, Luella D.	aged 23yrs 10mos 28das		7- 9-1880
KNIGHT-BROWN-WATKINS family marker			
, Joseph		1862	1930
, Fannie		1867	1942
, Claude		1891	1964
, Hessie R.		1894	1975
KNIGHT, Jeff		1859	1930
, Mollie	(same marker as Jeff)	1865	1958
, Fannie		1856	1887
, Vernon		1882	1884
, Carl B.		1896	1918
, Marion		10-24-1879	12-16-1956
, Lillian H.		2-10-1886	7-26-1951
, Clyde		1879	1938
, Pearl Downs	w. of Clyde (same marker)	1881	1917
, Chester E.		1888	1953
, Hattie		4- 3-1892	8-18-1926
KOENIGSTEIN, Nicholas J.		1877	1958
, Carrie B.		1879	19__
KREHBIEL, Oliver A.	WORLD WAR I	7- 1-1895	3-17-1965
KRING, Mar. E.		1933	1934
LAFOLLETTE, Beulah J.	infant d. of J. W. & R. M. LaFollette		1916
LAKE, Betty Belle		9-11-1894	3-24-1967
LAWRENCE, Willis Abner		9-20-1816	11-25-1907
, Albert		1877	1878
, Baby			1882
, Ollie T.	"Mother"	1872	1941
, William M.		1899	1966
, Mary S.	(same marker as William M.)	1901	No date
LEAKE, Rhelda D. Sarlls		1859	1958
LE COMPTE, Isaac N.		1846	1936
, Martha J. Hill		1850	1894
, John L.		1874	1918
, W. O. L.		1880	1940
, Raymond		1883	1894
, Josephine			12-21-1887
, Josephine	d. of J. S. & S. M.	1- 8-1854	8-16-1855
, Jesse J. M.		11-27-1878	3- 1-1903
, J. T.		2- 3-1909	7-14-1958
, Donald Ray	USAF KY KOREA	11-21-1934	1-21-1972

LEE, John W.	s. of Stephen & Elgiva Lee	10-21-1844	5-16-1849
, John D.		2-20-1883	11- 4-1949
, Fannie B.	(same marker as John D.)	1-31-1884	12-16-1972
, Gilbert C.		9-16-1902	1- 9-1977
, Lillian E.	(same marker as Gilbert C.)	9-16-1902	No date
LEITCH, Frank		1874	1946
, Georgia B.		12-22-1884	10- 1-1921
LEITZ, Anna Kelley		1904	1930
LESLIE, Lieut. Col. Walter W.	KY MED RES WWI	11-27-1868	12-10-1948
, Nellie Lindsey		6- 8-1864	10-27-1951
, Lawrence G.		1898	1965
LESSARD, Joseph A.		3-17-1890	5- 1-1972
, Ruth C.	(same marker as Joseph A.)	5- 4-1892	No date
LINDSAY, Mary Isabella	w. of Reuben C. Lindsay	4-23-1843	2-22-1865
LIST, George	aged 56yrs 11mos		9-10-1851
, Lucy C.		5-12-1810	3-17-1898
, Sarah Isabella	d. of George & Lucy List	1846	1852
, Mariam	aged 10yrs. 10mos.		1851
, John L.		8- 7-1843	4-22-1911
, Mary A. Giles	w. of John L. List	5-22-1852	8-19-1903
, Hillis		2-15-1877	1-26-1909
, Leonard Marvin		5-29-1879	12- 4-1897
, Lucy Catharine		3-21-1883	No date
, William Giles Jr.		1924	1926
, William Sr.	"Father"	12-12-1874	4-12-1956
, Pearl K. Bush		8-16-1887	6-23-1970
, P. H.		1872	1932
, Lucy E.	d. of P. H. & Bell F. List	11- -1860	7- -1882
, Minnie		1881	1948
, Hollis		1908	1947
, Henry B. Sr.	"Father"	1881	1944
, Lucy C.	"Mother" (same marker as Henry B. Sr.)	1887	No date
, Frank Smith		12-24-1887	11-13-1968
, Maude Graves		9-12-1893	No date
LOCKLAIR, Ellen		1873	1956
LONG, Dr. John		1- 9-1812	5-12-1885
, Nancy E.		1827	1911
, Dr. E. T.		7-25-1822	7-21-1898
, Luticia E.	(same marker as Dr. E. T.)	11- 2-1840	7-11-1914
, E. Willis	(same marker as Dr. E. T.)	4-14-1871	7- 6-1876
, Robert H.		1877	1935
, Annie C.		1875	1955
, Clarence	s. of J. & Lucy Long	10-12-1883	8-29-1894
, Sam V.		1882	1945
, Lola B.	(same marker as Sam V.)	1885	1971
, Lucian		1887	1956
, Effie Bishop		1888	1949
, Herman C.		6-17-1898	No date
, Ethel J.	(same marker as Herman C.)	2-19-1904	3-31-1975
, Howard C.		1925	1949
LOUDEN, Simpson		3-18-1833	5-25-1907
, Sarah	w. of Simpson (same marker)	No date	8- 6-1943
, John H.		10- 4-1854	4-11-1904
LOWDENBACK, Margaret Barr	w. of Wm. L.	1-20-1800	7-27-1894
, C. G.		2- 1-1825	4-13-1903
, Rachel B.	w. of C. G. L. (same marker)	2- 6-1825	2-24-1899
, David Barnes	(same marker as C. G. & R. B.)	11-26-1820	6-15-1904
LUCAS, Capt. H. K.		5- 6-1805	3-22-1857
, C. J.		2-24-1829	2- 5-1896
, Leanna E.	w. of C. J. Lucas	5- 2-1829	1-10-1892
, John H.		1-10-1864	12-28-1895
, Sarah A. E.		9-16-1871	1-14-1892
, Lucy		3- 1-1861	9-12-1913
LYLE, David B.		5-15-1767	5- 9-1841
, Nancy	w. of David Lyle aged 71yrs 4mos 16das		9- 8-1858
, Joshua R.		10-21-1809	7-19-1892
, Sallie M.	w. of J. R. Lyle	No date	2- 6-1835
, James P.		10-29-1844	12-20-1880
LYNCH, S. H.	"Father"	1838	1912
, Mary E.	"Mother" w. of S. H. (same marker)	1838	1912
, Will T.		1866	1935

Name	Remarks	Born	Died
, Nannie B.	(same marker as Will T.)	1870	1938
, Samuel		1890	1956
, Charlotte D.		1878	1954
LYONS, William		1854	1933
, Elizabeth	(same marker as William)	1871	19__
, Roscoe Coleman		1908	1975
, William Carroll		1904	1967
, Hettie Gale		2-18-1926	10-15-1926
, James H.		1865	1917
, Blanche B.		1876	1931
, John W.		1911	1961
, Infant	d. of J. H. & Blanche Lyons	No date	12- 2-1903
, Sol T.		1874	1949
, Alice B.	(same marker as Sol T.)	1874	1961
, Ruth Roberts		1887	1948
, William		1889	1972
, Ida C.	(same marker as William)	1900	No date
, Hobart		1900	1953
, Anna Lee	(same marker as Hobart)	1909	1937
, Mary Lou		1924	1951
, Woodrow		1912	1950
, Maymie Arnold		1915	No date
MADDOX, J. W.		3-25-1845	11-24-1898
, Mary A.	w. of J. W. Maddox	10-14-1849	9- 4-1885
, W. E.		2-13-1870	5-21-1899
, J. Pendleton		4- 9-1855	10-21-1902
Mattie B.	w. of J. Pendleton (same marker)	5-12-1857	6- 7-1928
, Herbert		1886	1950
, Ada Bright		1887	1963
, Cecil	KY PVT TANK SCHOOL	No date	7-28-1925
, John Thomas		1904	1964
, Kenneth G.	CO L 26TH INF	1924	1944
, Billy Allen		4-13-1962	4- 7-1966
MAGRUDER, William H.		1833	1909
, Maria W.	w. of Wm. H. (same marker)	1834	1913
, William H.		1868	1937
, Lillie E.		1875	1955
, Josiah B.		3- 3-1843	9-12-1918
, Artimecia	w. of Josiah B. (same marker)	10- 8-1847	1- 5-1929
, William P.	s. of J. and A. M.	10- 7-1879	4-16-1899
, Eugene O.		3-23-1885	5-25-1957
, Austia L.		3-24-1886	5- 7-1978
, P. J.		1844	1931
, Nellie F.	(same marker as P. J.)	1869	1889
, Patsy T.	(same marker as P. J.)	1846	1926
, Lucy J.	d. of P. J. and N. F. Magruder	9-25-1882	2- 1-1890
, Eugene H.	(small child's marker)	1913	1913
MAHAN, Luther R.		1890	1955
, Hattie B.	(same marker as Luther R.)	1892	1961
MAHONEY, Alford		11- 5-1876	9-29-1960
, Bessie May	(same marker as Alford)	5-15-1887	12-25-1965
, Flem	SPANISH AMERICAN WAR	12- 6-1878	1- 2-1962
, Bertha		1884	1918
, Leonard E.		5-16-1897	8-10-1972
, Ada Harlow		10-16-1897	No date
, Elliston		1899	1966
, Martha E.	(same marker as Elliston)	1893	1966
MALIN, Edwin R.		5- 6-1842	12- 8-1906
, Almeda	w. of Edwin (same marker)	8-28-1843	5-26-1927
, Susanne	w. of J. H. Malin	1- 9-1868	1-11-1901
, Ida Bibb		1867	1932
, Willie May Figg		1889	1966
, William Elzy	"Father"	1880	1953
, Almeda H.	"Mother" (same marker as Wm Elzy)	1882	1912
, Sarah C.	"Daughter"	1904	No date
MARION, John C.	KY SN USN	10-13-1935	8-23-1969
MARKEL, George W.		7-12-1893	2-11-1965
, Pearl Bohannon	(same marker as Geo. W.)	9- 3-1893	5- 6-1957
MARKHAM, James Davidson		1853	1945
, Sophronia	w. of Jas. D. Markham	11-16-1861	1-22-1890
, Norbourne	s. of Jas. D. & Sophronia M.	5-15-1881	11- -1902

Name	Notes	Born	Died
, Lucy	d. of Jas. & Sophronia Markham	3-26-1887	3-24-1897
MARKSBURY, Isaac Garrard		1875	1937
, Elizabeth Thomas	(same marker as Isaac G.)	1880	1953
MARSHALL, Sarah M.	"Mother" w. of Samuel P. Sm.	1823	1905
, Elizabeth	"Aunt" w. of Thomas F. Marshall	1828	1906
, Ida Lee	w. of Anthony Marshall	1875	1900
, Harold Hagan	s. of Anthony & Ida Lee M.	1899	1900
MARTINIE, Clyde		1888	1962
, Ada	(same marker as Clyde)	1889	1943
MARTIN, Lula Wells		1859	1910
, Jack		1890	1938
, Emma		1873	1943
, Pryor		1900	1951
, Annelle		1908	1929
MARX, Edwin D. D.		11-13-1885	10-28-1955
MASSIE, C. Milton		1852	1938
, Cassie B.	(same marker as C. Milton)	1859	1942
, George B.		1881	1908
, Willie	Infant s. of C. M. & C. B. Massie	1-21-1877	7-28-1878
, Erby		1887	1955
, Adeline K.	(same marker as Erby)	1889	1962
MAYS, Samuel W.		1849	1932
, Martha J. Ellis	(same marker as Samuel W.)	1859	1920
McALISTER, Henry B.		10-30-1887	12- 8-1957
, Ethel D.	(same marker as Henry B.)	3- 5-1897	12-27-1964
, Henry G.	KY CPL 139TH BN WWII	8-19-1926	7-21-1958
McCARTY, Tressye K.		1-27-1892	1-24-1972
McCONNELL, Isaac P.		11- 6-1813	1- 3-1853
,	(Fieldstone marks one grave)		
,	(White marble marker inscription worn smooth)		illegible
, Bettie S.	d. of I. P. & I. A. McConnell aged 10yrs 8 m 28d		3-12-1854
McDONALD, Robert Church		1879	1959
, Betty Pearl Hall		1883	1961
, Chester		1907	No date
McDOWELL, Lula D.	"Mother"	1868	1956
, Lelia	"Mother" (Parrish)	4- 4-1918	9-17-1961
, William Esq.	"Son" SGT USA Korea	6- 4-1934	10-17-1975
McGOWAN, Earl Ray	KY SI USNR WWII	1-15-1907	5- 4-1954
, May		1901	19__
, Baby McGowan			No date
McKEE, Joseph S.		1840	1921
, Angeline		1849	1943
, Willard		1874	1950
, Rosa Myrtle		1881	1912
, Bertha F.		1900	1905
MEAD, Fannie E.		7-23-1854	4- 7-1881
MEADOWS, W. J.		1-21-1823	5-23-1904
, Francis A.	w. of W. J. Meadows	9-17-1823	7-25-1879
MEFFORD, Luther M.		1882	1942
, Cynthia S.	(same marker as Luther M.)	1889	1937
MEREDITH,	Son of C. T. & Eva Meredith	No date	9-27-1893
MESSENGER, Corine Davis	"Mother"	1902	1972
MILLER, H. C.	"Father"	6-26-1862	10-24-1940
, Martha	"Mother"	7-16-1864	6-27-1954
, W. Fulton		1893	1970
, Blanche M.		1897	1958
MILLS, Sanford		1881	1969
, Maude		1880	1959
MITCHELL, John B.	"Father"	12-14-1835	11-13-1904
, Katherine Smith	"Mother" w. of John B.	1-17-1842	9-24-1917
, Newton S.		1841	1912
, Emma D.	(same marker as Newton S.)	1855	1919
, Herbert	s. of Newton & Emma Mitchell	1881	1901
, Clarence A.	"Father"	No date	7- 3-1957
, Amelia B.	"Mother" (same marker as Clarence)	No date	4- 3-1964
, James P.		1847	1917
, James Thomas		1860	1935
, Annie Lou Scobee	(same marker as Jas. Thos.)	1867	1940
, W. H.		1861	1930
, Helen S.		1867	1925
, J. B.		1902	1927

, Henry		1903	1930
, James E.		1894	1976
, Lena F.	(same marker as James E.)	1895	1945
, Alma Belwood		1893	1963
, I. N.		9-21-1909	10- 4-1969
MONIHON, John W.		5-10-1855	3-12-1913
, Capitola		10-29-1858	10-18-1918
, William H.		1883	1954
, Lucy B.	(same marker as William H.)	1887	1936
MONTFORT, Mary	aged 36yrs 2mos		10-21-1850
, Henry T.		8- 4-1820	5-20-1880
, Martha J. Kesler	w. of Henry T. M.	9-13-1826	6- 1-1912
, Henry		1- 4-1849	No date
, Mary T.	w. of Henry	2-22-1862	5-13-1920
, Annie	child of W. & Mary L. aged 2yrs 20days		10-16-1869
MOORE, Richard		5- 6-1823	2- 4-1905
, Lucy J.		3- 6-1839	2- 7-1933
, P. T.		7- 6-1866	5-15-1889
, Francis Asbury		4-16-1838	3-20-1893
, Lulie J.	w. of John W. M. "Mother"	1870	1908
, James R.		1857	1948
, Virgie H.	(same marker as James R.)	1857	1934
, J. Calvin		1858	1949
, Bettie S.		1855	1938
, Linden	s. of James R. & Virgie H. Moore	7-28-1885	4-21-1887
, Nannie C.	"Our Mother"	11- 7-1862	1- 9-1928
, George Drufal		3-22-1860	1-28-1938
, Elizabeth Clark	(same marker as Geo. D.)	4- 7-1865	4- 7-1936
, Nancy M.	"Mother"	1808	1887
, N. J.		1838	1931
, Mallie	(same marker as N. J.)	1841	1909
, Gertrude	d. of N. J. & Mallie Moore	9- 2-1870	9- 2-1870
, Hunter		1872	1930
, Myrabel		1870	1945
, Ole		1880	1973
, Bertha	(same marker as Ole)	1888	1968
, Minice	s. of H. F. & Cora Moore	No date	No date
, Pete		1883	1966
, Mary		1888	1944
MOORE-HALL-ESTES family marker			
, T. E.		4- 5-1865	9- 9-1932
, Ida B.		3-20-1872	2- 4-1939
MOPPIN, Lawrence		1941	1952
MORGAN, E. B.		10-19-1902	12-13-1965
, Nelle	d. of Wm. Morgan	1-27-1905	6-15-1905
MORRIS, John C.		4- 9-1841	4-23-1896
, Annie Bergen	w. of John C. Morris	1849	1923
MURPHY, Mary	w. of James L. Murphy	7- 4-1810	10-26-1862
MOUDY, John W.		1888	1959
, Annie B.	(same marker as John W.)	1889	1975
MYERS, Ralph Iona	PVT CO A 168 INF WWI	1-13-1893	7-26-1965
MYLES, John L.		1843	1919
, Fannie D.	(same marker as John L.)	1864	1909
, William N.		1899	1928
NASH, Elliott B.		1839	1930
, Lizzie B.	(same marker as Elliott B.)	1844	1921
, James Barnett		1873	1954
, Minnie Clubb		1873	1962
NEAL, Evelyn		9- 5-1850	12-13-1940
, Bernard E.		2- 4-1878	5-11-1970
, S. J.		1925	No date
, Anita Wood		1925	1964
NELSON, Patsy Jean	aged 1yr 2mos 20das		6- 6-1942
NEVEL, Mary		1820	2-13-1878
NEVILLE, Norman E.		1888	1974
, Nettie A.		1895	No date
NEW, Albert T.	PVT USA WWI	1892	1977
, Allie S.		1902	No date
, Martin		1901	1949
, Catherine K.	(same marker as Martin)	1907	1977
NEWKIRK, Henry T.	"Father"	8- 4-1820	5-29-1880

Name	Notes	Born	Died
, Martha J. Kesler	"Mother" w. of Henry T.	9-13-1826	6- 1-1912
, Katherine Montfort	"Mother"	1-21-1847	8- 3-1903
NEWMAN, Thomas	"Father"	10-12-1851	10- 3-1930
, Annie B.	"Mother" (same marker as Thos.)	7- 4-1870	6-26-1945
, Ray M.	PVT CO B 1ST INF ENGINEERS WWI	1901	10-10-1918
, Lillian M.		1888	1909
, Hallie		1898	1898
, Thomas Sidney		5-16-1874	5-17-1951
, Lillie Mae	(same marker as Thos. S.)	12-31-1878	2-23-1944
, Clarence E.		1- 3-1899	10-28-1934
, Sidney Thomas		11-21-1898	10-14-1966
, Herman Ray	FL USNR KY WWII	12-22-1907	5-13-1962
NOE, John J.		8-29-1867	1-11-1961
, Lucy B.	(same marker as John J.)	7-16-1867	11-16-1944
, W. H.		1871	1955
, Annie P.	(same marker as W. H.)	1879	1956
NORMAN, William V.		3-21-1888	10-31-1969
NUTALL, Bradford B.		1876	1956
, Price		2- 4-1881	4-17-1950
, Mary Yancey	(same marker as Price)	8-17-1889	11-18-1918
O'BRIEN, Michael		1878	1931
, Liza P.	(same marker as Michael)	1883	1973
, David		1896	1963
, Cordie	(same marker as David)	1901	No date
, David Jr.	PFC ARMY AIR FORCE WWII	11-12-1927	11-15-1975
, James	PFC CO A 37 ARM TANK BN KY WWII	9-30-1925	11-15-1952
, Cindy Carol		No date	5- 2-1952
, Robert		2-14-1898	9- 9-1957
O'BRIAN, Lelia Mae	aged 57yrs		4-17-1970
O' BRIEN, Pat		1946	1968
O'BRYAN, Adeline B.	w. of E. P. O'Bryan	12- 8-1825	9- 8-1897
O'KELLY, James		9-27-1844	1-26-1865
OLIVER, George W.		1890	1961
, Addie Mae	(same marker as George W.)	1892	1969
, Kenneth E. Jr.	(infant)	1947	1947
O'NAN, Samuel Cross		9-21-1878	10-10-1951
, Mary Stella	(same marker as Samuel C.)	7-29-1880	8-27-1961
, Herman		1903	No date
, Ollie		1902	1971
PARDO, R. L.		3-10-1864	7-29-1905
, Robert		1877	1926
PARKS, Alexander R.	PVT CO G 21ST REG KY INF CW	1845	1922
, John T.	"Father"	1868	1947
, Malissa L.	"Mother" (same marker as John T.)	1869	1943
, Montry		1888	1971
, Minnie	(same marker as Montry)	1890	1961
, Chester S.		1896	1953
, Mary T.		1909	1945
, Leslie B.		1-28-1899	8-17-1972
, Sallie A.	(same marker as Leslie B.)	1-12-1900	3-10-1978
PARR, Bruce		1896	1949
, Samie	(same marker as Bruce)	1899	19__
PARRISH, Benjamin	s. of N. & R. E. Parrish	3-12-1858	3- 8-1859
, George N.		1881	1926
, Nellie M.	(same marker as George N.)	1892	1973
, William L.	WWII (same marker as Geo. N)	6-17-1913	9-14-1973
, O. N.		1886	1928
, Elizabeth C.		1890	1933
, Lelia	"Mother"	4- 4-1918	9-17-1961
, Leslie E.		1890	1934
, Mary E.		1893	No date
PAYNE, Joel		1835	1915
, Celista	(same marker as Joel)	1853	1930
, Pearl S. E.		1877	1956
PENDLETON, Jesse		1848	1915
, Clemmar R.		1852	1937
, J. T. P.		1-14-1891	11-18-1896
, Margaret		8- 9-1897	8-18-1904
, Fred		1893	1919
PENN, Susan S.		6-24-1840	10-27-1913
PEPPER, Presley Nevil		10- 4-1804	9- 2-1881

, Eleanor W.	w. of Presley P. N. (same marker)	1812	1904
PERKINSON, Lovie Banta		1881	1969
, Moody		4-10-1893	7-27-1947
, A. N.		1868	1949
, Mary E.		1863	1926
PERRY, Mary M.		12-18-1829	8-31-1897
, Grover C.		1884	19__
, Mary Angeline H.	(same marker as Grover)	1891	1955
, James William	"Father"	4-11-1883	2-18-1964
, Mae Mitchell	"Mother"		
, Alvin P.	PVT 562 AAA AW BN CAC KY WWII	1-31-1909	9-20-1966
, Elmo Dean	"Son" CPL INF KY WWII	5-27-1918	2- 2-1945
, Eugene	s. of W. E. & Ella Perry	1-12-1883	12-16-1892
PEYTON, Robert Sr.		1869	1912
, Florence B.	(same marker as Robert Sr.)	1876	1953
, Virginia	(same marker as Robert Sr.)	1906	1907
, Robert Jr.		1902	1928
, Elva Audry	(same marker as Robert Jr.)	11-29-1905	8-25-1971
, Waunita Dorten	(same marker as Robert Jr.)	1900	1950
POLK, Gertrude	w. of J. B. Polk	3- 2-1888	4- 5-1919
POLLARD, William	"Father"	3-11-1823	8-20-1901
, Marinda	w. of Wm. "Mother"	9-23-1830	No date
, Eliza		1830	1904
, John H.	"Father"	1869	1933
, Lizzie Dora	w. of J. H. Pollard	11-24-1871	6-29-1898
, William Lewis	"Father"	1854	1938
, Clementine	"Mother" (same marker as Wm)	1859	1935
, Lorena		1886	1964
, George T.		186_	illegible
, W. H.		1881	1947
, Maude K.		1877	1964
, Carrie F.		18__	illegible
, Mary E.			illegible
, Elizabeth			illegible
, Arthur	s. of G. T. & C. P.	9- 7-1898	6-29-1899
, Marrie	d. of G. T. & C. P.	10-26-1893	7-29-1895
, Alonzo		1877	1952
, Mollie K.		1883	1970
PORTER-ALEXANDER-BOTTOM family marker			
, Sarah A. Porter		1878	1951
POYNTER, Charles N.		1893	1975
, Grace H.	(same marker as Charles N.)	1896	1962
PRICE-ROBERTS family marker			
, Newton Price		8-11-1882	5- 9-1967
, Vina Price		1-2[illegible]-1884	5- 2-1929
, Ben Nathan Price		6-22-1914	4- 5-1974
PRICE, Sallie Johnston		4- 9-1881	5- 6-1975
, Mary B.		1876	1959
, Joseph	(same marker as Mary B.)	1904	1944
PROCTOR, Edward Lee		1872	1926
, Florence Radcliffe		1875	1923
, Richard R.		7-25-1904	6- 5-1971
, Helen Agatha		1902	1903
, Mary Bernice		1910	1916
, Ida Helton			No date
PRYOR, Nannie Q.		1856	1934
PURVIS-McALISTER family marker			
, Elmer		12- 9-1888	2-13-1973
, Mary M.		11-18-1891	4-16-1968
, Lloyd Cecil		7-31-1912	No date
, Minice Jones		3- 3-1901	4-28-1972
, Laura Arnold		11-27-1904	1- 1-1977
QUISSENBERRY, Rev. William H.		2- 5-1823	10-16-1881
, Caroline	"Our Mother"	6- 6-1821	2- 3-1892
, Cora Lee	d. of R. & Amanda D. Quissenberry	5-22-1881	3-18-1885
QUISSENBERRY-MASSIE family marker			
, Breck Quissenberry		1855	1936
, Mary Jane Quissenberry		1862	1924
, Katie H. Quissenberry		1897	1948
, Perlie	d. of S. B. & M. J. Q.	6- 2-1892	8-13-1892
QUISSENBERRY, James Henry	"Father"	1883	1937

Name	Remarks	Born	Died
, Ida Belk	"Mother" (same marker as Jas. H.)	1891	1929
RADCLIFFE, James W.		1844	1909
, Nancy J.	(same marker as James W.)	1845	1934
, Mary		1869	1884
, Samuel		1872	1940
, Hardin		1880	1964
, Joseph	"Dad"	1885	1942
, James R.		1866	1927
, Fannie B. Flood		12- 1-1876	10-10-1961
RANDOLPH, Nettie		1847	1932
RANDOLPH-WALLACE family marker			
, N. A.		1886	1933
, Ida W.		1888	1961
RANKIN, Martha Ellen		1836	1930
, Isabella	w. of M. C. Rankin	1-22-1849	7-31-1889
, Jimson P.		1851	1916
, Jennie Highfield	w. of Jimson P. Rankin	1856	1932
, Willard		1869	No date
, Josie	(same marker as Willard)	1867	1919
, M. P.		1870	1946
, Mishie S.	(same marker as M. P.)	1870	1925
, Hickman		1899	1937
, Maude	(same marker as Hickman)	1900	1976
, Abner	"Father"	1868	1937
, Linnie Floyd	"Mother"	1876	1922
, Pauline	"Daughter"	1907	1946
, Grover C.	PVT CO D 109 MACH GUN KY WWI	6-18-1891	7-14-1969
, Ethel James		6-28-1894	8-20-1969
RANSDELL, Edward Porter		1877	1967
, Jessie Tucker	(same marker as Edward P.)	1880	1968
RAWLINGS, Margaret Ann		1836	1916
RAY, Walter Lillard	IND WWII	5-12-1913	3- 5-1973
REED, John A.		1815	1871
, Martha J.		1824	1893
REESE, Maurice		1895	1922
REEVES, Willis		12-20-1860	No date
, Ida May	w. of Willis Reeves	3-20-1867	5-10-1906
, Laurinda	d. of Willis & Ida May R.	9-23-1888	7-13-1908
, J. Leonard		1891	1956
, Eula W.		1893	No date
, J. S.		1830	1940
, Forest McKee		1897	1958
, Sarah Blair	(same marker as Forest McKee)	1897	1975
, Silas L.		1- 3-1857	3- 3-1941
, Flora	w. of Silas L.	10- 6-1872	5- 3-1900
, Boyd W.		5- 1-1892	1- 9-1924
REYNOLDS, William Wesley		1-20-1928	2-25-1928
RICE, Mattie Tuck	"Mother"	1848	1935
, Essley T.	WWI	12- 1-1895	6-17-1954
RIDGEWAY, Thomas F.		1847	1923
, Edmonia	(same marker as Thomas F.)	1856	1931
, Johnnie B.	s. of T. F. & E. Ridgeway	4- 6-1885	11- 3-1887
, Preston B.	"Husband"	7- 5-1850	3-27-1889
, Ida Ridgeway Key		No date	1-10-1907
, Samuel R.		1882	1970
, Sallie B.	(same marker as Samuel R.)	1882	1975
RITCHIE, Nellie Hall		8- 3-1906	2-27-1936
RINER, J. T.		1854	1932
, Sarah J.	w. of J. T. Riner	7- 4-1860	7- 8-1902
, Cora Wilhite	w. of J. T. Riner "Mother"	1881	1950
	Infant of J. T. & S. Riner		3- 4-1897
, S. B.		12-10-1878	2-15-1962
, Sallie Hammond		8-29-1870	3-10-1949
, A. M.		2-26-1847	2- 9-1897
, William Samuel		2- 7-1852	10-11-1929
, Mattie Hudson	(same marker as Wm Samuel)	2-12-1866	3- 5-1921
, Bertha Madison	(same marker as Wm Samuel)	6-12-1890	5- 6-1903
, Ida May	(same marker as Wm Samuel)	8-31-1896	1-27-1902
, Mattie Isabel	(same marker as Wm Samuel)	10- 2-1902	8-25-1903
, Grace	(same marker as Wm Samuel)	3- 4-1899	11-25-1899
, Jessie Todd	(same marker as Wm Samuel)	9-11-1891	4-30-1892

, Myrtle Wood		1881	1939
ROACH, Joseph	"Grandfather"	1842	1928
, Eldora	"Grandmother"	1845	1924
ROBERTS, G. W.	"Father"	2- 1-1838	12- 1-1894
, S. E.	"Mother" (same marker as G. W.)	11-20-1847	1906
, M. A.	"Daughter"	12-25-1866	7-18-1886
, A. E.	"Daughter"	3-15-1869	No date
, C. T.	"Daughter"	9- 3-1872	No date
, S. R.	"Daughter"	1-24-1888	No date
, W. H.	"Boys"	2-11-1880	1915
, L. B.	"Boys"	11-11-1882	1937
, G. W.		11- 3-1842	8-29-1907
, James	"Father"	12-18-1849	5-18-1917
, Lou Ann	w. of James "Mother"	No date	No date
, Tyra		9-14-1884	7-16-1966
, George W.		1849	1934
, Alice Gordon	(same marker as George W.)	1853	1937
, J. W.		8-30-1854	12-16-1907
, Bette	w. of J. W. (same marker)	8- 9-1847	2-17-1926
, L. Dow		1852	1932
, Mary J.	(same marker as L. Dow)	1855	1932
, William P.		1855	1919
, Ellen	(same marker as William P.)	1860	No date
, William H.		1854	1922
, Cordelia	(same marker as William H.)	1860	1943
, Caldwell		1893	1966
, Newton		1861	1927
, Susie A.	(same marker as Newton)	1868	1932
, Harrison		1862	1935
, Mary J.		1863	1916
, Sandford		1866	1927
, Hallie J.	(same marker as Sanford)	1868	1968
, Herbert	s. of Sanford & Hallie J. Roberts	1889	1891
, John W.		5-23-1868	4-14-1930
, Norah	w. of John W. (same marker)	9-17-1874	12-21-1908
, John	"Husband"	1873	1940
, Laura C.	"Wife"	1872	1964
, J. Jasper		1873	1941
, Annie M.	(same marker as J. Jasper)	1877	1961
, Paul		1907	1929
, Lloyd		1904	1950
, Florence	(same marker as Lloyd)	1910	1950
, Fannie		1870	1963
, Sol		1873	1945
, Carrie		1873	1920
, Michael		1868	1939
, Kate	(same marker as Michael)	1871	1948
, William V.		5-13-1890	12-16-1964
, John		10-25-1835	7-19-1910
, Sarah	w. of John (same marker)	1- 7-1842	12-12-1909
, Burbon	(same marker as John & Sarah)	1871	19__
, Mary	w. of Burbon (same marker as Burbon)	1869	19__
, Edmond T.		11-24-1869	3- 3-1948
, Mary Frances		1917	1948
, Joe E.	"Father"	1-14-1874	2- 9-1928
, Gurtie	"Mother"	7- 6-1878	2-16-1912
, Maudie	"Sister"	2-15-1912	7-17-1914
, Margaret		1-25-1927	2- 2-1929
, Arthur L.		1878	1941
, Bertie B.	(same marker as Arthur L.)	1881	1972
, Jonathan		1861	1914
, Mary E. Rowlett	w. of Jonathan	1861	1905
, George	"Father"	8-26-1879	11- 5-1952
, Ida Kelly	"Mother"	5-26-1884	3-23-1955
, James C.		1893	1970
, Annie Belle		1894	1919
, Eloise		1917	1918
, James William		10- 8-1913	2-27-1974
, Jema Lee		1916	1917
, Jesse		1891	1962
, Lacie	"Mother"	1892	1965

Name	Notes	Born	Died
, Clay		1888	1956
, Ruth Botts		1885	No date
, Alvia P.		1891	1969
, Eugenia M.	(same marker as Alvia P.)	1896	1977
, Lou B.		1887	1922
, Mabel	(same marker as Lou B.)	1890	1921
, Ora Lee		1889	No date
, Rachel E.		1885	1976
, Edna Margaret		1919	1963
, Lena Arnold		1895	1970
, Fred		1895	No date
, Myrtle Searcy		1895	1953
, Herman S.	PVT US MARINE KY WWI	5-17-1896	11-12-1970
, Chester Lee	FL USN RF KY WWI	2-16-1897	9-27-1951
, Brenda Darlene		No date	1951
, Clarence A.		1897	1971
, Florence N.	(same marker as Clarence A.)	1900	1978
, Sam McKinley		9-20-1896	3-21-1974
, Bertha R.	(same marker as Sam McKinley)	3-23-1908	No date
, Preston		1898	1940
, Helen	(same marker as Preston)	1905	1965
, George Thomas		1900	1977
, Thelma Hundley		1902	No date
, George Thomas		1937	1937
ROBERTS-STIVERS family marker			
, Morris Roberts		2-18-1897	11-25-1973
, Ruth C.		2-16-1896	No date
ROBERTSON, W. R.		1836	1916
, James		9-16-1841	3-29-1890
, John T.		1865	1951
, Fannie G.		1869	1953
, James C.		1889	1952
, Grace		1891	1964
, Virginia		1890	1929
, Sarah E.		1871	1955
, Edward R.		1876	1965
, Maude	(same marker as Edward R.)	1885	1975
, Rosa E.	w. of B. B. Robertson	5-25-1872	9- 9-1912
, Ruth		9-10-1909	6-30-1911
, Robert L.		1- 6-1867	7-29-1929
, Lizzie W.	(same marker as Robert L.)	12-12-1865	1-13-1919
, Annie W.		1838	1922
, George E.	s. of R. L. & L. W. Robertson	7-22-1891	1-17-1894
, Ernest G.	s. of R. L. & L. W. Robertson	5-28-1894	5-12-1895
, Wesley	"Father"	1869	1927
, Jennie B.	"Mother"	1873	1958
, Jimmie		1891	1959
, Elliott		1897	1970
, Sadie	(same marker as Elliott)	1909	No date
, Oscar		1876	1964
, Susan		1881	1949
, Cecil W		1911	1925
, Thelma Shephard		1902	No date
, Vivian Oscar		1901	No date
, Corine		1-31-1922	10- 6-1935
, Leonard		1898	1973
ROBERTSON-BATTERTON family marker			
, J. M. Robertson		1865	1939
ROBINSON, June		11-14-1885	1- 1-1947
, Lizzie B.	(same marker as June)	11- 6-1888	8-28-1974
, Ernest M.		1908	1971
, Louise S.		1915	No date
RODGERS, Lewis Thomas	SPANISH AMERICAN WAR	6-24-1865	9-23-1956
, Stella R.	(same marker as Lewis Thomas)	1888	1967
, Hardin		2- 9-1872	6-16-1959
, Goodlow W.		9-29-1859	2-18-1898
RUCKER, Moses		1838	1898
, Mary E.	w. of Moses Rucker	1840	1899
, Pinkie Hall	d. of Moses & Mary Rucker	1871	1897
, Rhoda	(same marker)	1874	1935
, Eliza M.	(same marker)	1877	1898

Name	Notes	Born	Died
, William H.		4-27-1850	3- 4-1882
, Ira J.		1880	1954
, Malisse	(same marker as Ira J.)	1884	1959
, Oscar		1877	1931
, Anna D.	(same marker as Oscar)	1882	1966
, Morrison	PFC 148 GEN HOSP KY WWII	1-26-1914	7-24-1948
RUSSELL, Hazel Banta		1888	1913
SANDERS, Maryline	w. of H. M. Sanders	1862	1908
, Nathan		1878	1917
, Sallie B.	w. of Nathan (same marker)	1878	1962
SANFORD, L. W.		4- 3-1849	6-20-1929
, Susan M.	w. of L. W. Sanford	10- 4-1847	10-25-1902
, Julia	w. of L. W. Sanford	8- 2-1852	2- 8-1921
, Mary G.	w. of L. W. Sanford	1862	1926
, Grover A.	PFC HQ CO 326 FA KY WWI	3-26-1888	2-15-1959
, Perry S.	COMMODORE U.S.C.G. ALA	11-30-1889	5-15-1963
, William Benjamin		12-24-1914	1- 2-1939
, Lonnie		No date	No date
, Carrie Aynes		No date	No date
SCHOOLER, A. B.		4- 5-1830	6-18-1905
, Mary	w. of A. B. Schooler	No date	12- 1-1883
, Bonbne		7-18-1882	3-20-1906
, Alma	w. of J. L.	1- 4-1855	6- 5-1885
, Emit B.		7-14-1896	5-15-1899
, Ada Bush		11-23-1875	11-18-1958
, Abb		1881	1958
, Bess L.	(same marker as Abb)	1888	1956
, John W.		3-27-1861	7-12-1908
, Fannie	(same marker as John W.)	4-20-1861	5-13-1940
, Josie Beverly		1907	No date
, Russell G.		2-26-1914	11-16-1914
SCHRAMM, W. A.		1843	1921
, Annie	w. of W. A. (same marker)	1851	1935
SCOBEE, Robert		1844	1915
, Jennie		1850	1928
, John W.	"Father"	1845	1913
, Bettie	"Mother" (same marker as John)	1856	1937
, Bain		1880	1966
, Hester	(same marker as Bain)	1887	1970
, Russell M.		1877	1951
, Estelle B.		1880	1967
SCRIBER, Chester		1891	1937
SCRUGGS, Marcellus		10-24-1840	7-30-1918
, Amanda	w. of Marcellus	4-16-1851	2-14-1947
, Flournoy		1870	1953
, Pryor		1900	1928
, Julia	w. of Leslie	12- 8-1877	4- 5-1903
SCUDDER, William H.		1875	1937
, Laura Johnston	w. of William H.	1871	1934
SELF, John R.		1877	1950
, Annie, L.	(same marker as John R.)	1879	1934
, Leo G.	CPL QM DS CO KY WWII	12-10-1920	4- 5-1968
Eurith Black		2-28-1929	No date
SEWELL, William H.		1848	1929
, Joanner, H.		1858	1933
, Charles S.		1876	1964
, Christen		1888	No date
, John W.		1849	1915
, Mary A.	(same marker as John W.)	1853	1948
, David C.		1864	1941
, James Clifton	PVT 1 CL 162 INF 41 DIV KY		11-15-1925
, J. T.		12-26-1867	1-28-1964
, James B.		1867	1935
, Lizzie James	(same marker as James B.)	1877	1958
, Ballard T.		No date	12- 8-1898
, William F.		1870	1945
, Mary Annie		1874	1949
, Delores K.		1921	1950
, Joe Will		1873	1947
, Fannie L.		1884	No date
, Preston		5-13-1875	3- 5-1938

, Janie M.		4-25-1881	2-13-1934
, Edward C.		1883	1953
, Alice W.	(same marker as Edward C.)	1890	1976
, Albert Morton	WWI	2-10-1892	5- 3-1961
, Irvine B.		1923	1926
, George Winfred		4-22-1895	2-21-1974
, Ella Wainscott	(same marker as Geo. W.)	1-29-1894	No date
, George Ralph	(same marker as Geo. W.)	7- 9-1917	No date
, Albert	married Florence 2-9-1924	1899	19__
, Florence	(same marker as Albert)	1901	1968
, Fannie B.		1899	19__
, Eugene	PVT 159 DEPOT BRIGADE KY WWI	3- 7-1894	4-22-1970
SHADWICK, Ad		11- 3-1894	7-18-1967
, Novella Woods		11-15-1897	7- 7-1976
SHANNON-BATES family marker			
, James W. Shannon		1872	1948
, Nellie G. Shannon		1873	1970
SHANNON, Forest		2- 6-1890	4-15-1961
Mattie	(Same marker as Forest)	5- 4-1888	No date
SHARP, L. F.		8- 2-1830	3-31-1895
, John		1870	1946
, Mattie	(same marker as John)	1881	1922
, Earl		1903	1975
, Morgan		1886	1960
SHAW, John	"Father"	1846	1918
, Mary F.	"Mother" (same marker as John)	1849	1935
, Budy	"Son" (same marker as John)	1869	1955
, Silas W.		1851	1929
, Mary E.	(same marker as Silas W.)	1855	1937
, Lillie E.		1880	1949
, Samuel Herbert	WWI	7-18-1890	2-12-1966
, S. N.		1854	1924
, Kate		1862	1944
, Susie E.		1887	1977
, Linden		1871	1933
, Lula		1880	1961
, James W.		1877	1948
, Anna B.	(same marker as James W.)	1883	1951
, Owen A.		1894	1977
, Lizzie D.	(same marker as Owen A.)	1895	1931
, Bertha James	w. of Owen Shaw	1909	1955
, James Q.		1-12-1919	2-28-1973
, Vivian E.	(same marker as James Q.)	10- 9-1922	No date
, Hugh Urban		1898	1977
, Ethel Hall	(same marker as Hugh Urban)	1903	No date
, Luther H.		1879	1968
, Irene	(same marker as Luther H.)	1876	1941
, Louella B.		4-24-1899	3-20-1965
SHELTON, J. W.		1862	1944
, Corda H.	(same marker as J. W.)	1865	1955
, Joe		1881	1960
, Adella	(same marker as Joe)	1887	No date
, Rhoda	w. of Joe Shaw	12-13-1890	2-15-1909
, Danny	WWI	3-31-1894	7- 2-1957
, Anna Scriber		1895	1962
, Oda Miki		1891	1976
SHIPP, Walter Garey	married Athla Shaw 1913	1889	1972
, Athla Shaw	(same marker as Walter Garey)	1894	1969
SHIPMAN, George F.	"Father"	12-27-1845	1-16-1896
, Mattie	"Mother"	9-30-1849	6-26-1926
, William D.		1874	1940
, David L.		10- 8-1862	1-16-1914
, Eliza F.		1873	1964
, David I.	s. of David & Eliza Shipman aged 21yrs. 6mos. 15das.		
SHOCKENCY, J. W.		12- 4-1819	8-13-1891
, M. A.	(same marker as J. W.)	8- 2-1827	8-16-1902
, John B.		6- 3-1849	5- 1-1918
, George		1851	1925
, Robert		4-28-1853	12- 2-1918
, Emily		1858	1941

Name	Remarks	Born	Died
, Almeda	w. of Richard Shockency	10-12-1838	7- 4-1919
, Mariam	d. of R. & A. S.	9-17-1857	5-11-1886
, Richard F.		1863	1929
, Minnie Bergen		1861	1946
, Infant	s. of R. F. & M. B. S.	11-13-1893	11-27-1893
SHUCK, John	aged 78yrs		1- 3-1858
, Prucilla	w. of John Shuck aged 72yrs		12- 6-1852
, R. H.	aged 89yrs 10 mos 20das	4 2-1817	2-20-1908
, Maria S.	w. of R. H. Shuck	10-11-1824	12-18-1868
, Martha E.		11-21-1830	4- 3-1900
, James T.		9- 4-1851	3-19-1863
, Charles A.		9-27-1858	10- 8-1932
, Mattie E.		11-27-1858	10-12-1925
, John Y.	s. of (illegible)	10-11-1846	5- 8-1847
, Stewart R.		1890	1944
, Sarah P.	d. of (illegible)		5-25-185_
, Richard M.		1861	1924
, Peter	brother of Richard M.	1846	1907
, James W.		6-14-1829	3-15-1906
, Rebecca	w. of James W. (same marker)	3-12-1832	No date
, Edmon T.	s. of J. W. & R. S.	2- 1-1887	12-24-1890
, Frank		1842	1911
, Emily	w. of Frank Shuck	1841	1911
, Andrew		11-14-1845	No date
, Jane	w. of Andrew Shuck	11-18-1844	1-30-1909
, Fountain		10-29-1871	3-18-1889
, Charles		7-30-1879	10-21-1909
, Katie B.		11- 1-1850	6-11-1921
, George William		10- 1-1853	4-11-1923
, Nannie T.	(same marker as Geo Wm)	7-23-1869	12- 6-1954
, Joseph F.		1855	1931
, Harriet B.	(same marker as Joseph F.)	'859	1941
, Hershal J.	s. of J. F. & H. F. Shuck)	2- 4-1897	10- 8-1900
, Ernest I.		1877	1916
, Mary M.	(same marker as Ernest I.)	1882	1975
, John Thomas		1858	1946
, Lula Smoot		1868	1962
, Alice	w. of J. W. Shuck	5- 4-1862	10- 1-1902
, S. Curtis		1879	1947
, Jennie Stivers		1883	1961
, Glady	Infant of Curtis & Jennie Shuck		10-22-1913
, Lloyd L.	WWII	2-15-1909	1-27-1968
, J. C. W.	"Our Baby"		No date
, Harvey M.		4- 7-1862	8-16-1913
, Martishia		1867	1942
, Rhomba	d. of H. M. & M. Shuck	11-28-1884	12-21-1901
, Everet T.	s. of H. M. & M. Shuck	1- 7-1898	10- 7-1899
, Eli		1864	1918
, Lucy Ellen		1873	1948
, Albert M.		1898	1944
, John W.		2-25-1874	11-30-1902
, Nannie P.	"Mother"	1878	1928
, Ernest M.		1881	1949
, Price A.		1904	1967
, Leona C.	(same marker as Price A.)	1903	No date
, W. T.	s. of E. & L. Shuck	1902	No date
, William	PVT USA WWI	7-13-1896	11-10-1975
, Virgie G.	(same marker as William)	10-20-1900	8-18-1976
, George Reuben		2-21-1897	6-18-1939
, Martha Riner		7-25-1893	3- 8-1974
, Everett G.		8-27-1924	5-24-1960
, Jean M.		5-24-1926	No date
, Nannie B.		12- 8-1884	3-10-1953
SIMPSON, Leafie	"Mother"	1891	No date
, Ruby S.	"Daughter"	1921	1940
SKELTON, Henry		10-26-1866	No date
, Mattie T.	w. of Henry	6-24-1871	6- 2-1913
SKIDMORE, Noble E.		1884	1963
, Lillian R.	(same marker as Noble E.)	1888	1969
, Ralph J.		9- 4-1900	No date
, Hallie W.		8-25-1895	2-14-1974

Name	Notes	Born	Died
SKILES, Dee		9-22-1888	7- 6-1965
, Clara C.		8-21-1889	10-16-1969
SLEMMONS, James W.		1824	1903
, Sallie E.		1832	1911
, Alice		9- 8-1873	11-21-1876
, Lee	s. of J. W. & S. E. S.	11-22-1866	2- 2-1882
, George	s. of J. W. & S. E. S.	12- 8-1859	3-26-1896
, Henry C.		1864	1916
, Annie T.		11-27-1862	1-25-1896
, J. D.		1852	1934
, Amelia Lawson	w. of Jos. S. "Mother"	10- 8-1840	2-11-1894
, Charles W.		1868	1906
, Elizabeth	"Mother" aged _	No date	11-21-1881
SMITH, R. M.		10-23-1834	10-28-1912
, Fannie	w. of R. M. (same marker)	2-15-1853	8-15-1907
, Robert Thomas	(same marker as R. M.)	9-28-1904	3-19-1910
, Nannie E.	"Mother"	6-15-1837	11- 1-1922
, George W.		1881	1971
, John T.		1841	1905
, W. V.		1851	1925
, Jane E.	w. of W. V. (same marker)	1851	1938
, Frank E.		1853	1926
, Anne S.		1868	1958
, Frank B.		8- 8-1858	12- 4-1895
, Ida Gale		1860	1940
, Nancy	w. of J. B. Smith	9-15-1867	9- 9-1888
, J. B.		4-22-1865	9-17-1941
, Mary E.	w. of J. B. Smith & d. of Monroe & Sue Flood	1-28-1866	10-11-1895
, James G.	aged 44yrs		3-16-1893
, Fannie E.		11- 8-1861	11- 4-1958
, Clarence		1883	1959
, Barbara B.	(same marker as Clarence)	1890	1974
, Calvert		12- 5-1876	10- 5-1970
, Flurry		1875	1956
, Elizabeth	(same marker as Flurry)	1873	1963
, Kirby		9-18-1883	4- 8-1973
, Hallie Scott	(same marker as Kirby)	11-25-1890	No date
SMITH-THURMAN family marker			
, Ernest William Smith		1882	1945
, Bessie Hall Smith		1884	1947
SMITH, Charlie L. B.	"Father"	1882	1953
, Sarah Head	"Mother" (same marker as C.)	1882	1923
, Imogene B.	"Daughter"	1913	1915
, Mayre B. Miley	"Daughter"	1915	1949
, John William		1898	1960
, Margaret Cox	(same marker as John W.)	1906	No date
, John William Jr.	s. of J. W. & M. C. S.	6- 7-1931	2-26-1933
, Paul S.	2ND LIEUT INF KY WWI	8- 6-1895	6- 4-1971
, Henry Dale	FI USNR KY WWII	11- 9-1915	10-24-1955
SMITHER, Jake		1877	1943
, Alpha	(same marker as Jake)	1885	1942
, Kate	w. of Thos. S.	3-11-1856	11-13-1917
, Levi		1875	1930
, Rena	(same marker as Levi)	1874	1964
, Edmond	s. of Levi & Rena S.	3-20-1902	7-16-1902
, Ernest D.		1898	1969
, Letha S.	(same marker as Ernest D.)	1897	19__
, Mary Belle	d. of Ernest & Letha S.	11- 1-1917	2- 1-1921
SMITHERS, Boss		11-13-1885	11- 4-1960
, Minnie M.	(same marker as Boss)	9-24-1889	No date
, Lucille		1911	1923
, Rhetta L.		1896	1977
SMOOT, John W.		7-23-1848	10- 8-1911
, Medora	w. of John W.	1-18-1850	5-23-1926
, Margaret M.	(same marker as John)	10-29-1878	8-29-1904
, Nellie B.	(same marker as John W.)	11-16-1874	10-19-1949
, Thomas	"Father"	2-28-1822	2-10-1902
, Lucy	w. of Thos. "Mother"	5-17-1841	No date
, Reuben		1873	1945
, Daisy		1878	1958

Name	Remarks	Born	Died
, George		1876	1945
, May		1878	1942
, Jack T.	2ND U.S. CALVRY SPAN AMER W	1883	1948
, Delya C.		1882	1961
SNEED, Coleman H.		1860	1942
, Bena G.		1865	1944
SNIDER, Peggy O'Brien		9- 9-1930	10-22-1936
SPARKS, Robert		2-15-1777	4-10-1831
, Isabella	w. of Robert Aged illegible		4-19-1837
, Betsy Valatta	d. of R. & I. S.	6- 9-1819	12- 1-1841
, Phoebe	d. of R. & I. S.	illegible	7-13-1863
, Clarence		5- 7-1808	7-12-1876
, John F.		5-26-1799	9-21-1871
, Patsy	w. of John F. S.	9-26-1803	12-20-1836
, Eleanor G.		5- 7-1808	7-12-1876
, George T.	s. of John & Nellie S.	6- 5-1838	4-18-1863
, Eliza A.	w. of H. Sparks "Mother" Aged 76yrs		4-24-1886
, Lucy J.	w. of Wm. & ___ illegible		1879
, John A.		1863	1939
, Mollie E.	(same marker as John A.)	1864	1948
, Harry Lee	WWI	11-24-1888	5-21-1973
, Vera Thomas	(same marker as H. L.)	2-25-1891	6-26-1977
, George W.		1853	1946
, Emma F.	(same marker as George)	1862	1941
, Delbert L.		1881	1961
, Valdia J.	(same marker as Delbert)	No date	No date
, William Iverson		1884	1950
, Mariam Adams		1890	1965
, Harry Lee Jr.		9-22-1928	1-10-1931
SPEED, Jane		1842	1923
, Willard		1874	1935
, L. A.		1878	19__
, J. W.		8-21-1866	No date
, Ophelia D.		10-26-1870	7-31-1945
SPILLMAN, P. T.		1861	1946
STALKER, Marshall N.	"Father"	1847	1934
, Mattie D.	"Mother" (same marker as M.)	1849	1931
, Willie		1885	1926
, Carl		9-22-1890	11- 1-1895
, Opha L.		1888	1968
, Rosa V.	(same marker as Opha L.)	1890	1964
, Charles M.		1883	1964
, Anna W.	(same marker as Charles M.)	1887	19__
, Goodwin	S SGT USA	1919	1974
STAPLETON, G. W.		1856	1934
, Julia Montfort	w. of G. W. S.	12-13-1858	9-24-1902
, Mattie Bula	d. of G. W. & Julia S.	8-18-1882	10- 5-1902
, Joseph W.		1878	1962
, Nancy White	(same marker as Joseph)	1880	1946
STASEL, Clifford C.	WWII	1- 7-1907	11- 3-1969
, Ruth B.	(same marker as Clifford)	1-30-1911	No date
STEPHENS, Ida May		1867	1944
STEWART, Lucy A.	"Mother"	9-29-1845	7-21-1936
, John W.		1885	1966
, Daisy F.	(same marker as John W.)	1893	No date
STEENSON, Valentine	"Husband"	1891	1950
, Eula	"Wife"	1903	No date
STEVENS, Charles		No date	1938
, Mattie		1888	1958
, Hansford B.	WWII	3- 1-1905	1- 9-1973
STINSON, Edna Elizabeth	w. of H. C. Stinson	7- 5-1890	4- 1-1928
STIVERS, C. P.		5- 5-1845	7- 2-1919
, Sarah	w. of F. P. Stivers	10- 8-1853	7-19-1882
, Infant	s. of F. P. & S. I. Stivers	7-19-1882	9-19-1882
, T. S.		1859	1912
, Alice E.	w. of J. T. Stivers	8- 9-1855	2-22-1881
, Winfield Scott		1862	1935
, Sarah Elizabeth	(same marker as W. S.)	1869	1941
, Lewis W.		1866	1949
, Jane E.		1876	1946
, W. B.		1869	1922

, James M.		1871	1959
, Sarah C.	(same marker as James M.)	1868	1942
, Herman		1899	1919
, Linden		1877	1960
, America	(same marker as Linden)	1881	1956
, James		1877	1952
, Gertrude		1876	1936
, Marie Hughes		1900	1939
, Arthur L.		1878	1967
, Katie	(same marker as Arthur L.)	1888	No date
, Olie S.	married Bettie M. 4-4-1906	1879	1972
, Bettie May	(same marker as Olie S.)	1880	1969
, John H.		1883	1965
, Sallie Shaw	(same marker as John H.)	1886	1961
, Dallas C.		1887	1973
, Bessie H.	(same marker as Dallas C.)	1889	1969
, Daisy L.		11-21-1888	11-12-1900
, Sidney		1860	1919
, Melissa	(same marker as Sidney)	1863	1916
, Wm. F.	child of S. & M. J. S.	10- 1-1894	10- 5-1895
, James B.	child of S. & M. J. S.	10- 1-1894	9-15-1895
, Bettie A.	d. of S. & M. J. S.	6- 8-1889	8- 4-1899
, Emory		7-26-1875	No date
, Malinda A.	w. of Emory	6-25-1876	3-30-1917
, J. C.		4-18-1901	1-21-1956
, Sibbie		5- 8-1904	12-11-1970
, H. Byron		1887	1953
, Louise S.	(same marker as H. Byron)	1892	1958
, John H.		1890	1954
, Grace J.		1895	1945
, Forest D.		1917	1937
, James C.		1888	1964
, Pearl Shelton	(same marker as Jas. C.)	1894	1965
, Harvey		1894	1936
, Geneva	(same marker as Harvey)	1892	1937
, Boyd		1891	1952
, Mary Ethel	(same marker as Boyd)	1892	1970
, Ollie J.		12-30-1915	No date
, Christine Bright	(same marker as Ollie)	9-11-1912	2- 3-1974
, Minice J.		1894	1962
, Maude	(same marker as Minice)	1898	1969
, Luke		1898	1941
, Ralph	PVT CO C 50 INF KY WWI	4-14-1894	10-13-1966
, Mable		7-15-1902	No date
, Ramey C.		1898	1969
, Sherley B.		1896	No date
STIVERS-BAKER family marker			
, Edgar W.		1888	1976
, Effie B.		1895	19__
STIVERS-ROBERTS family marker			
, Randolph		1-12-1921	No date
, Nora Alice		2-18-1923	No date
STONE, Thomas C.		1854	1917
, Adeline B.		1865	1931
, Willie Ellis		1892	1968
, Sibyle Hughes		1898	1952
, I. T.		1899	1973
, Rebecca	(same marker as I. T.)	1903	No date
, Harvey Lee		1931	1934
, Harvey E.		6- 2-1872	7-29-1900
STROKER, Francis O.		5-18-1867	6-26-1959
, Rhelda B.	(same marker as F. O.)	9-17-1875	4- 1-1948
SUTHERLAND, Charles A.		2-17-1883	5-14-1963
, Dora Miles	(same marker as C. A.)	1887	1967
, Estle		1885	1955
, Charlotte C.		1891	19__
SUTTON, Leander		1862	1940
, Cordia	(same marker as Leander)	1871	1944
, George	"Our Dad"	6- 8-1898	10-18-1969
, Ray S.		8-27-1913	3-24-1928

, Ronald L.		No date	1949
SWEENEY, Patrick		1855	1943
SWINDLER, Robert Sanford		1885	1965
, Ollie	w. of R. S. Swindler	1883	1935
Lucy Hundley		1884	1966
TACKETT, Alex		1869	1952
, Nannie G.	(same marker as Alex)	1864	1933
, Thomas J.		1871	No date
, Annie B.	(same marker as Thomas J.)	1869	No date
, Charles E.		1906	1942
TATE, Margaret F.	w. of W. A. Tate	1837	1899
TATUM, Louella B.		1889	1964
TAYLOR, Henry T.		1879	1943
, Elizabeth C.	(same marker as Henry T.)	1883	1959
, Ernest		1894	No date
, Lillie F.	(same marker as Ernest)	1895	1971
THOMAS, M. Shelby		1855	1941
, Emma Jane		1859	1927
, Ubert John		1891	1930
, Robert S.		1860	1937
, Martha Beverly		1860	1943
, Margaret Carter		7- 3-1888	1-21-1972
, James Hiner		6-28-1889	8-28-1930
, John C.		1853	1931
Mattie Corley		1857	1940
, Sam		1864	1949
, Icey		1881	1949
, Infant	son of Sam & Icey T.		3-21-1907
, Joe C.		1865	1925
, Pearl I.		1873	1971
, Mike		1-22-1873	10-13-1967
, Emma W.	(same marker as Mike)	10-24-1878	12- 7-1964
, Robert E.	PVT US MARINE KY WWII	9-17-1926	3- 8-1945
, James C.		1866	1953
, Betty	(same marker as James)	1874	1949
, Kenneth C.		1906	1949
, Spencer C.		1873	1903
, Georgia		1875	1960
, Melvina Bibb	"Mother"	1882	1963
, Gayle B.	married Effie 1911	4-21-1889	2-12-1965
, Effie S.	(same marker as Gayle)	3-11-1891	No date
, Raymond		186[illegible]	1964
, Maude	w. of Raymond Thomas	189[illegible]	1912
, Albert R.	aged 10das		11-24-1911
, Ana Roberts	(same marker as Raymond)	1898	No date
, Estel C.		1898	1967
, Evalina Curtright		1903	1954
, James C.		1900	1950
, Ethel C.	(same marker as James C.)	1904	19__
THOMASON, J. S.		5-10-1849	6- 5-1908
, Mildred		1- 7-1851	11-30-1898
, Mamie		4- 7-1854	4-18-1908
THOMPSON, Mary		1833	1921
, Berry		1842	1909
, Elizabeth	w. of Berry Thompson	1843	1909
THRELKELD, Cap		1839	1877
, Fannie	(same marker as Cap)	1842	1906
, Morgan		1866	1933
, William R.		1906	1908
, W. S.		3-16-1873	1-29-1946
, Mary Harding		12- 2-1875	2-16-1941
, George M.		1878	1957
, Mary J.		1885	1940
, W. M.		9-24-1835	8- 9-1907
, Mollie Wills		1849	1937
, John W.		1882	1958
, Martha A.		1890	1970
, G. B.	s. of W. M. & M. W. T.	9- 9-1887	10- 2-1887
THURMAN, Joe		3- -1847	9- -1931
, Nancy G.		1850	1926

Name	Remarks	Born	Died
, Mary E.		3-14-1871	12-19-1950
, Gabreill		5- 1-1878	4-17-1899
, Walter	s. of E. W. & Anne		No date
, Georgia A.		5- 7-1873	9-30-1897
, J. B.		2-16-1880	6-11-1900
, Press R.		1876	1955
, Alpha E.	(same marker as Press R.)	1875	1951
, Ira D.		9-26-1892	12-12-1972
, Mattie Ellis	(same marker as Ira)	6-23-1892	4-17-1960
THURMAN-SMITH, family marker			
, Oswald Thomas Thurman		1900	1976
, Mary Smith Thurman		1903	1935
THURMOND, Cassie		1894	1957
, Wm. P.	CPL AAF KY WWII	9-10-1921	10-24-1972
TIBBALS, L. Eugene		1880	1953
TOON, James F.		1876	1963
, Clara B.	(same marker as James F.)	1882	1971
TOTTEN, Mattie May		1874	1910
TRUMAN, George M.		1893	1969
, Margaret	(same marker as George M.)	1891	No date
TUCKER, Cornelius B.		1851	1929
, Jennie M.	(same marker as Cornelius)	1854	1930
, Metta L.		1878	1952
, Anna May		1884	1954
, Lorinne B.	s. of C. B. & Jennie T.	11-16-1894	11-20-1894
, James H.		1846	1915
, Lula Smith	(same marker as James H.)	1861	1942
, Oscar	s. of J. H. & L. S. T.	11-29-1886	11-16-1890
, Mary T.	d. of J. H. & L S T	3-27-1889	11-20-1890
TURNER-FLOYD family marker			
, Edward Mason Turner		1873	1957
, Nancy Elizabeth		1896	1974
, Nancy Edwina	infant	No date	No date
TYREE, Sa		1888	No date
, Lucy	(same marker as Sa)	1896	1951
UNDERWOOD, Dr. William L.		1849	1929
, Fannie Threlkeld	(same marker as Dr. Wm.)	1850	1939
, James Sprigg	s. of Dr. Wm. L. & F. T. Underwood	12-14-1872	10-16-1878
,	a small marker illegible		
, Frank		1872	1919
, Mary V.	w. of Frank A. Underwood	7- 4-1876	8- 5-1898
, Cecelia		1877	1964
, Susanna E.	w. of R. W. Underwood	11- 1-1885	8-29-1908
, John A.		1876	1929
, Bertha R.		1877	1969
, James H.		1879	1945
, Sibbie K.		1880	1958
, Ben F.		1884	1956
, Claude C.	(same marker as brother Ben)	1875	1955
, Samuel T.		2-27-1882	2- 5-1963
, Laura B.	(same marker as Samuel)	9-20-1887	11- 9-1973
, Frank W.		1907	1974
VANCE, Robert W.		1883	1939
, Florida C.		1880	1969
VALLANDINGHAM, Emma		1865	1948
VANDAGRIFFT, Mahala		9-30-1826	12-30-1907
VORIES, Albert	PA RIFLE REG 1775-1783 aged 76yr 11mos 10das		2-18-1830
, Cornelius A.	aged 79yrs.		6- 8-1863
WADE, Sarah A.		illegible	illegible
, Oscar P.		1864	1950
, Bettie Cox	(same marker as Oscar P.)	1867	1925
Clancie M.	"Father"	1890	1978
, Francis	"Son" (same marker as Clancie)	1913	1977
, Linnie C.		1895	1969
WAINSCOTT, Alfred		1860	1913
, Alfred Jr.	(same marker as Alfred)	1896	1918
WAITS, Robert H.		1875	1949
, Laura	(same marker as Robert H.)	1882	1961
, Mary Emma		1915	1923
, Robert S.		4- 1-1910	No date

Name	Note	Born	Died
, Ada B.	(same marker as Robert S.)	9-23-1911	10- 9-1969
WAKEFIELD, Anne Harding		10-25-1886	1-27-1939
WALLACE, William R.		1849	1926
, Martha J.		1849	1930
, J. P.		1854	1932
, E. R.		10-11-1851	5-26-1925
, Bettie		8- 2-1863	9-23-1946
, Minnie F.	d. of Perry & Rachel W.	12- 5-1876	7- 6-1966
, Ida B.	d. of Perry & Rachel W.	1878	No date
, Annie E.	d. of Perry & Rachel W.	1885	1952
, Della M.	d. of Perry & Rachel W.	1881	1919
, Milt		1887	1972
, Kate		1886	1950
, Clarence A.	PVT USA KY WWI	8-19-1893	4-17-1973
, Bessie B.	(same marker as Clarence)	1913	1973
, Lynda Ann		1945	1945
, Otis		1882	1974
, Jennie	(same marker as Otis)	1887	1969
WALLIS, Ebenezer R.		1895	1965
, Margaret O.	(same marker as Ebenezer)	1894	1970
WALTERS, Thomas B.		5-15-1871	2- 2-1904
WALTON, Harry G.		8-22-1870	10-29-1901
WASH,, M. F. Lowdenback	w. of T. E. Wash	8-22-1852	5- 9-1890
WASHBURN, W. E.		1863	1938
, Eliza B.	(same marker as W. E.)	1862	1956
, Pearl	d. of W. E. & E. Washburn	1883	1915
, Ed		1895	1973
, Daisy	(same marker as Ed)	1899	1965
, John T.		1898	1973
, Eva	(same marker as John T.)	1897	No date
WATKINS, L. B.		5-28-1877	No date
Geneva Lee	(same marker as L. B.)	8-25-1903	5-22-1904
, I. L.	(same marker as L. B.)	7-17-1878	No date
, Christie		1879	1941
, Rachel Johnson		1883	1950
, Arthur		1881	1948
, Stella V.		1885	1953
WAY, James P.		1887	1962
WEAKLEY, Thomas C.		4-23-1898	1-17-1972
WEAVER, Herman	S SGT 1324 SER UNIT ILL WWII	2-24-1909	9- 3-1945
WEBB, Barnett		1884	1943
, Clara	(same marker as Barnett)	1887	No date
WEBSTER, Edgar O.		1883	1913
, Myrtle M.	(same marker as Edgar O.)	1885	1936
, Jesse C.		10- 1-1911	1- 7-1912
WELCH, W. O.		1872	1949
, Sallie	(same marker as W. O.)	1880	1962
, Marjorie		1948	1972
, Sonnie		1901	1977
, Mary Susie	(same marker as Sonnie)	1911	No date
WELLS, Lafayette		1834	1899
, Sallie Lyle		1838	1913
, John W.		1832	1918
, Carolyne	w. of John W. (same marker)	1832	1927
, Edward P.	s. of J. W. & C. Wells	1872	1903
, J. S. Richard	s. of J. W. & C. Wells	6-11-1870	5-21-1890
, I. T.		1838	1927
, Nancy	w. of I. T. Wells	12-11-1840	8-14-1913
, Edgar		1860	1947
, W. B.		1864	1930
, David		1862	1928
, Annie R.		1886	1960
, James B.		4-26-1841	1-18-1899
, Amanda T.		7-10-1842	9-15-1903
, George C.		1858	1942
, Edna E.	(same marker as George C.)	1859	1932
, George F.	(same marker as George C.)	1893	1895
, Lottie F.		1892	1893
, Infant	son of George C. & Edna E. Wells	7-13-1889	12-10-1890
, Rev. W. T.		1862	1940

Name	Notes	Born	Died
, Elma P.	w. of W. T. Wells	2-11-1867	1-22-1892
, John Tilden		12-26-1876	12-31-1960
, John J.		1864	1939
, Katie P.	(same marker as John J.)	3-24-1860	1936
, Mabel Clare		1895	1922
, Annie Lou	d. of J. J. & K. P. Wells	9-11-1889	2- 5-1890
, Emory	"Father"	1869	1928
, Minnie Rankin	w. of Emory "Mother"	1873	19__
, Anna McKay	d. of Dr. N. B. & Anna E. Wells	9- 6-1874	2- 9-1877
, Paul		1-17-1879	4- 3-1966
, Josephine H.	(same marker as Paul)	10-30-1889	8-18-1963
WELTY, Fannie Stone		8-20-1876	1-31-1958
WENTWORTH, Herman		1880	1964
, Creda E.		1886	1963
WHALEY, Robert T.		1887	1954
, Amanda W.	(same marker as Robert T.)	1889	1963
, Joseph Hoyt	CO X BSM USN KY WWII	10-24-1919	9- 1-1973
WHEELER, Kelley B.		1890	1919
, John M.	s. of G. W. & A. S. Wheeler	7- 5-1904	7-11-1904
WHITE, Charles H.		1847	19__
, Sallie E.	(same marker as Charles H.)	1860	1930
, M. E.		7-22-1838	No date
, Mary E.	w. of M. F.	7- 3-1841	5-20-1898
, Neville B.	"Father"	1863	1938
, Myrtle M.	"Mother"	1865	1949
, Edward R.		1857	1941
, Edward B.	(same marker as Edward B.)	1964	No date
WILBORN, Charley		8-18-1855	12-25-1906
, Georgie	w. of Charley	10- 3-1859	9- 4-1899
WILDER, Wilson		1868	1961
, Amanda E.	(same marker as Wilson)	1872	1946
, Margaret W. Walker	(same marker as Wilson)	1892	1955
WILHITE, Martha Ann	w. of J. S. Wilhite	10- 4-1851	4- 3-1903
, Veener		1875	1966
, Mary B.	(same marker as Veener)	1882	1973
WILHITE family marker			
, J. W.	"Father"	12-17-1853	10-22-1914
, Belle	w. of J. W. "Mother"	6-22-1860	10-19-1927
, Otho		1-15-1880	No date
, Leonard		5- 3-1881	No date
, Orvie		9-29-1888	
, Irena		8- 9-1878	8- 8-1900
, Forest		10-23-1895	4-19-1897
WILHITE family marker			
, J. B.		4-17-1862	No date
, Lizzie	w. of J. B.	10-11-1866	7-19-1905
, Mable		2-17-1881	No date
, Omer		5- 2-1886	No date
, Ethel		2-27-1889	No date
, Nellie		9- 1-1890	No date
, Earl		5-21-1893	No date
, Grace		2-27-1897	No date
, Herschel		1-15-1903	No date
, Mable	d. of J. B. & L. Wilhite	2-17-1884	6-24-1899
WILHITE, John		1868	1953
, William	"Father"	1878	1918
, Sue E.	"Mother"	1881	1969
, John W.	aged 72yrs		No date
, Fornie			1937
, Bettie A.	(same marker as Fornie)		1945
, Arthur		1-14-1872	4-22-1959
, Odia B.	(same marker as Arthur)	10-24-1877	7- 9-1965
, Flossie Mae		10-31-1901	10-15-1918
, Otho		1880	1918
, Lula E.		1882	1959
, Leonard Y.		5- 3-1881	12-28-1964
, Ethel R.	(same marker as Leonard Y.)	1- 8-1883	7- 7-1972
, Alfred T.		10-18-1840	2- 7-1919
, Martha W.	(same marker as Alfred T.)	3-10-1847	7-11-1915
, Ernest		11-16-1883	1-29-1965

Name	Notes	Born	Died
, Bertha M.	w. of Ernest (same marker)	5-14-1880	3- 6-1919
, Orvie O.		1888	1966
, Mary S.		1900	No date
, Sell		1889	1958
WILHOITE, Arthur		1883	1963
, Nettie S.		1885	No date
WILLIAMS, W. G.		3-23-1805	4-23-1899
, Charles W.		12-25-1825	5-18-1906
, Mildred Perry	w. of Charles W.	10-18-1830	3-12-1907
, B. F.		5-16-1826	8-11-1894
, Nancy	w. of B. F. Williams	10-20-1832	1- 8-1892
, George W.		9- 9-1830	1-26-1892
, Martha A.	(same marker as George W.)	6-23-1835	7-16-1892
, Mattie Lou	(same marker as George W.)	4- 3-1888	4-22-1889
, Thomas L.		1856	1922
, Annie E.		1862	1939
, Jack		1897	1918
, Georgia		1890	1965
, John L.		1879	1961
, Sallie S.		1880	1960
, Fred	CPL U.S. MARINE CORPS KY WWI	4-10-1882	5- 8-1956
, Reuben C.		1883	1961
, Pearl D.	(same marker as Reuben C.)	1895	1955
WILLIS, Oather	(same marker as Oather)	9-27-1886	3- 3-1973
, Nora O'Nan		3- 2-1884	6-18-1965
, Lillian I.		1885	1954
WILLS family marker			
, John E.		11-30-1822	2- 6-1892
, Nancy	(same marker as John E.)	10-18-1824	7-17-1894
, Mary Faancis	(same marker as John E.)	1843	1844
, Sarah Ann	(same marker as John E.)	1844	1858
, Fielding	(same marker as John E.)	1852	1866
, Eliza Jane	(same marker as John E.)	1858	1869
, Robert G.	(same marker as John E.)	5- 2-1861	11- 8-1900
, Rebecca A.	(same marker as John E.)	6- 2-1848	5-10-1902
, Amanda Pollard	(separate marker)	8-27-1860	10- 6-1904
WILLS family marker			
, G. W.		9- 4-1824	2-11-1903
, Mattie E.	(same marker as G. W.)	4- 2-1830	9- 4-1888
, Sarah A. Wade	(same marker as G. W.)	12-25-1826	11- 7-1846
, Rebecca	(same marker as G. W.)	1-23-1834	2-20-1867
, Mary J. Cropper	(same marker as G. W.)	illegible	illegible
, Sarah Elizabeth	d. of G. W. & E. W.	4- 5-1856	9- 4-1886
WILLS family marker			
, J. W.		1-27-1846	7-24-1910
, Mary C.	w. of J. W. (same marker)	3-24-1860	6-24-1901
, Bell C.	w. of J. W. (same marker)	7-17-1858	9-30-1915
, Sallie R.	d. of J. W. & Mollie Wills	8-15-1880	7-28-1890
WILLS, James F.		1854	1926
, Emma L.	(same marker as James F.)	1858	1950
, J. T.		4-26-1850	12-15-1927
, Sallie G.	w. of J. T.	2-21-1864	7- 5-1922
, G. W.	(a large marker)	No date	No date
, Callie	(same marker as G. W.)	2-28-1864	1-28-1920
, Daisey	(same marker as G. W.)	3-18-1885	No date
, Prentice V.	(same marker as G. W.)	7-28-1886	6- 6-1903
, John T. Jr.	(same marker as G. W.)	No date	No date
, Willie		1874	1954
, Ella D.		1876	1923
, Willie Pearl		3- 9-1905	8-23-1905
, Cleopatra		7- 9-1893	5- 5-1933
, Milton		1851	1927
, Lucy	(same marker as Milton)	1852	1929
, Selena May	d. of Milton & Lucy	5- 7-1878	2-15-1883
, Bessie	d. of Milton & Lucy	8-28-1880	9- 3-1883
, Fred D.		1869	1965
, America O.	(same marker as Fred D.)	1870	1962
, Ernest C.		1874	1944
, Lucy Wood		1877	1960
, Mary E.		1899	1957

Name	Notes	Born	Died
, Corinne		1901	1926
, Clyde Gano		1883	1952
, Elizabeth	w. of Clyde Gano	1891	1919
, Bertha Hall	w. of Clyde Gano	1892	1974
WILLSON, O. B.	"Father"	1844	1924
, Anna E.	"Mother"	1846	1928
, Clarence		1868	1928
, Flora		1873	1877
, Lillian		1876	1876
, Otho		1880	1934
, Mary		1883	1885
, Annie		1886	1890
, Bertie		1891	19__
WILSON, Sallie E.		5-31-1839	8-27-1907
, Narcissus Quisenberry W.	"Mother"	10-17-1847	7- 7-1933
, John B.		10-30-1873	5-19-1923
, Robert S.		7-20-1871	2-18-1894
, James R.		5- 6-1876	11- 3-1903
, W. T.		9-24-1880	4- 5-1907
, Eugene D.		1877	1963
, Mary P.	(same marker as Eugene D.)	1885	1924
, Porter		1911	19__
, Marie	(same marker as Porter)	1913	1941
, Bertha		1882	1950
, George	infant s. of J. M. & Sadie	11-18-1892	11-29-1892
, Alex		1896	1953
, George M.		1870	1955
, Pearle T.	(same marker as George M.)	1874	1906
,	Infant of G. M. & P. W.	1906	1906
, Paul R.		1900	No date
, Nettie B. Nuthall		1905	1929
, Elizabeth Kesler		6-23-1908	10-25-1946
WINTERS, John W.		1879	1952
, Ora M.		1883	1940
, Charlie C.		1902	1972
WITTWER, Emil		1889	No date
, Miriam		1889	1943
WOIRHAYE, Rose Brown		1873	1948
WOOD, Thomas		2-27-1835	2-22-1900
, Susan	w. of Thomas Wood	No date	No date
, Stephen	"Father"	3-28-1848	6-22-1929
, Mary E.	"Mother" (same marker as Stephen)	9-20-1849	5-25-1912
, J. T.		8- 6-1839	3-17-1909
, Elizabeth		1- 5-1844	8- 5-1915
, James H.		1878	1930
, Frank T.		1880	1943
, Eva L.		1882	1972
, John E.	"Father"	1864	1925
, Mary T.	"Mother" (same marker as John E.)	1868	1924
, Roberta		1862	1947
, A. Chester		1895	1930
, James S.		12-29-1872	7- 9-1918
, Mattie E.	(same marker as James S.)	1-16-1869	9-21-1960
, R. S.	"Sammy"	9-10-1910	No date
, Luther Samuel	(same marker as R. S.)	6- 2-1930	10- 3-1931
, Lucille E.	(same marker as R. S.)	10- 4-1911	No date
, Martha Jean	(same marker as R. S.)	2-23-1932	No date
, George T.		1872	1903
, Nannie W.	(same marker as George T.)	1876	1964
, Gilbert		1896	1966
, Ruth E.		1-23-1894	1-23-1911
, Will		4-10-1874	7- 7-1921
, Julia Ann	w. of Will Wood	8- 4-1874	9-29-1913
, Luther		1884	1958
, Clara Neal	(same marker as Luther)	1876	1963
, Stephen Arthur		1882	1966
, Myrtle Shuck	(same marker as Stephen A.)	1882	1968
, Montea		1883	1960
, Effie Mitchell	(same marker as Montea)	1887	1957
, Raymond Lee		1911	No date

Name	Remarks	Born	Died
, Marie Clubb	(same marker as Raymond L.)	1911	No date
, Raymond Bryan	s. of Raymond & Marie W.		8-22-1933
, Earl D.	PVT 1st INF KY WWII	4-27-1926	4-18-1945
, Morris Thomas		5- 5-1890	9- 5-1973
, Nell Graves	(same marker as Morris)	12- 1-1890	9-16-1967
, Mary Isabell Clubb		3-29-1897	4-16-1964
, Janet Lee		No date	12-15-1950
, Helburn H.		1897	1947
, Ethel B.	(same marker as Helburn H.)	1904	No date
, Earl Morris	PFC KY WWII	10-14-1923	3- 3-1972
, Pauline McCarty	(same marker as Earl)	1917	No date
WOODS, Alex		10- 3-1864	4-23-1956
, Emma		12-10-1878	1- 3-1954
, O. T.		6-20-1881	10-12-1919
, Flora		12- 7-1881	10-19-1953
WOOLDBIDGE, Alice	w. of L. P. Wooldbidge	2- 2-1877	11-17-1902
WRIGHT, Rev. Henry C.		5- 3-1848	2- 1-1914
, Margaret Ann		1858	1953
, Henry Rand		1892	1957
, Julian H.		1886	1910
, Margaret V.	w. of Marvin W. Wright	1894	1921
, Ernest Henry		9- 8-1916	4-15-1970
YEAGER, Preston Sr.		10-27-1922	12-14-1964
YOUNG, John H.		5-10-1844	6-21-1923
, Deliah G.	(same marker as John H.)	5-26-1851	11-18-1940
, Billie	s. of E. M. & Mabel Young	No date	No date
, Earl L.		1876	1970
, Lillie	(same marker as Earl L.)	1876	1959
YOUNT, Mattie M.	"Mother"	9-25-1833	10-27-1899
, Linden A.		1882	1943
, Bessie H.		1887	1975
, Mattie L.	d. of G. W. & N. I. Yount	5- 4-1878	11-17-1890

82. "The Highlands" Callaway Family Cemetery, Ky. 22 E. of Eminence.

Name	Remarks	Born	Died
CALLAWAY, Col. John	who departed this life in the 50th year of his life		
(Family record, born 8-25-1775)			7-31-1825
, Martha	wife of Col. John Callaway	9-24-1778	10-27-1831
, J. S.	(John Samuel Callaway)	illegible	illegible
(Family record, born 5-22-1807, died 8-15-1853)			
, Martha	(Durrett, wife of John Samuel)	illegible	18__
(Family record, born 10-11-1810, died 5-8-1887)			
, Richard Callaway		10-30-1798	12- 7-1846
COLEMAN, Infant	daughter of S. W. & M. E. Coleman		10-29-1859
KRACK, Mary K.	daughter of Dr. J. A. & M. E. Krack, aged 11mos.		10-10-1851
Pieces of other stones were illegible)			

83. Ricketts Family Cemetery, Between Campbellsburg and Newcastle West of Kentucky 55 & 421 on Beasley Lane.

Recorded by Mr. and Mrs. Richard Radcliffe of LaGrange.

Name	Remarks	Born	Died
RICKETTS, Elder Robert W.		8-21-1794	1- 1-1856
, Sallie W.	w. of R. W. Ricketts	3-20-1796	5-11-1889
GOODE, Martha V.	leaving 4 children	10-16-1823	2-25-1853
FOREE, Cordelia Ricketts	w. of C. F.	6- 7-1817	12- 6-1897
, Dr. John T.	only son C. & C.	10-26-1837	8-15-1883

ADDITIONS

HENRY COUNTY CEMETERIES

The following names were omitted from the Henry County cemetery records previously published.

13. Smithfield Public Cemetery.
By Smithfield Baptist Church.

CRABB, Samuel C.	a. 36 yrs.	3-22-1809	10-20-1845
EBER, John		5-22-1810	2-22-1876
GOODRIDGE, Martha C.	d. of F. H. & E.	4-18-1831	11-19-1832
THOMPSON, Sophia	Mother	11- 4-1795	3- 1-1880
, P. W.		9-12-1818	8-19-1910

17. Morris Graveyard.
N of Hwy. 157 between New Castle and Sulphur, 150 yds E of Sulphur Public Cemetery.

MORRIS, Benjamin F.		4- 9-1851	9- 9-1890
, Sister Baby	d. of W. J. & M. M.	6-18-1874	
, Willie J.	d. of D. & A. M.	12- 9-1858	8-13-1866
, Willie Pearl	d. of W. J. & M. M.	5-24-1877	11-16-1877
, Infant	son of Sallie A. & H. H.	2-19-1883	2-19-1883
, Infant	son of J. A. & Nannie B.	1- 9-1878	1- 9-1878
, Willie	son of C. L. & M. Martin	2-26-1871	6-29-1888
, Lottie May	d. of M. F. & Mintie Shaw	12- 5-1881	11-15-1884

23. New Castle Public Cemetery.
11/2 m N of New Castle.

FOREE, Peter		1745	1844
, Peter G.		4- 6-1851	1-21-1884
, Susan Roberts	w. of Thos. P.	7-13-1832	1-23-1879
WOIRHAYE, Wm. B.	s. of J. M. & L. F.	5-24-1861	4-18-1879

58. Campbellsburg Public Cemetery.

FERGUSON, Maggie A.	w. of J. W.	10- 2-1840	1-27-18__
STAPP, Robert A.		1861	1888

www.ingramcontent.com/pod-product-compliance
Ingram Content Group UK Ltd.
Pitfield, Milton Keynes, MK11 3LW, UK
UKHW020135250726
13967UKWH00002B/663